Balanced in the Wind

Balanced in the Wind

A Biography of Betsey Mix Cowles

LINDA L. GEARY

A Western Reserve Historical Society Book

LEWISBURG
Bucknell University Press
LONDON AND TORONTO: Associated University Presses

Associated University Presses
440 Forsgate Drive
Cranbury, NJ 08512

Associated University Presses
25 Sicilian Avenue
London WC1A 2QH, England

Associated University Presses
P.O. Box 488, Port Credit
Mississauga, Ontario
Canada L5G 4M2

The paper used in this publication meets the requirements of the American National Standard for Permanence of Paper for Printed Library Materials Z39.48-1984.

Library of Congress Cataloging-in-Publication Data

Geary, Linda L., 1955–
    Balanced in the wind.

    (Western Reserve Historical Society Publication; no. 170)
    "A Western Reserve Historical Society book."
    Bibliography: p.
    Includes index.
    1. Cowles, Betsey Mix, 1810–1876.   2. Pioneers—Ohio—Western Reserve—Biography.   3. Western Reserve (Ohio)—Biography.   4. Western Reserve (Ohio)—History.   5. Social reformers—Ohio—Western Reserve—Biography.
    I. Title.   II. Series.
    F497.W5C794   1989   977.1'38   [B]   87-46434
    ISBN 0-8387-5154-7 (alk. paper)

Western Reserve Historical Society Publication Number 170

PRINTED IN THE UNITED STATES OF AMERICA

FOR

"Gammie"

Contents

Acknowledgments

I wish to convey my appreciation to the following individuals for their contributions to this work. The fact that this study was made possible at all is due to the Cowles family who, through many generations, preserved their family papers and correspondence. Betsey Cowles's great-grandniece, Margaret Cowles Ticknor of Austinburg, is to be commended for her foresight in donating the papers to the American History Research Center at Kent State University. The papers are now easily accessible for further study, and I wish to thank the Center's staff for their cooperation and assistance. Mrs. Ticknor also was kind enough to guide me around the old Cowles homestead and to show me many of the family relics and portraits still on display in the original parlor setting.

Professor Frank L. Byrne of Kent State University guided me through the early stages of preparing this manuscript and continued his encouragement during the years that passed. His patience and optimism are very much appreciated. My thanks also to Larry Rubens of Kent State for his superb photography in reproducing the illustrations that appear in this work. The final draft of this manuscript was generally accelerated with the skilled technical assistance of Anindya Bose and the constant reassurance from Bani Bose that it would soon be finished.

My parents, Bud and Pepper Folck, and all of my family were, although miles away, with me always in spirit. My gratitude to them will never end. Finally, throughout this project I have enjoyed the unwavering support of my husband, Jim. His contribution is truly beyond words.

Balanced in the Wind

1
The Ohio Country

BETSEY Cowles grew up in the early nineteenth-century "Ohio Country," and her earliest memories were of pioneers and of a vast western wilderness. She was born in 1810, to a large Connecticut family whose ancestors were rooted in New England. Her great-great-great-grandfather, John Cole, emigrated from England to Massachusetts in 1635, soon married, and eventually moved with his five children to Farmington, Connecticut. Thereafter, all of Betsey Cowles's lineal paternal ancestors were born and made their livelihoods in that small Connecticut town. Her great-great-grandfather, Samuel Cowels, who changed the orthography of the family name, raised ten children on the family's Farmington property. His eighth son, Captain Isaac Cowles, became an extensive landholder, married three times, and fathered twelve children including Betsey Cowles's grandfather, Ezekiel, in 1721. Ten of Ezekiel's children became Betsey Cowles's New England aunts and uncles; one, Giles Hooker Cowles, was her father.[1]

Betsey Cowles's direct New England relatives were by no means poor, but they were nonetheless members of a hardworking merchant-farmer class with little or no higher education. Giles Hooker Cowles was the first known member of her immediate family to enter a ministerial vocation after having graduated from Yale College in 1789. In 1791, the Reverend Doctor Cowles was licensed to preach, and traveled in the following year to Bristol, Connecticut, for his first installment with the Bristol Congregational Church. There, he enjoyed an eventful seventeen-year ministry and became greatly admired by his fellow Congregationalists as a faithful, able, prudent, and zealous pastor.[2] He held several successful revivals, added numerous members to the Congregational fold, and ambitiously graced the previously modest meetinghouse decor with a steeple and a bell.[3] Troubled frequently by "salt-rheum" and a leg affliciton that caused him to limp, the minister nevertheless expanded his pastoral duties to

include visiting and praying with individual families and school-
children.

Giles Hooker Cowles was not only a learned, pious, and faithful
pastor, but also a devoted family man who undoubtedly passed on his
religious fervor and educational bent to his children. In 1793, barely
four months after his ordination at Bristol, Cowles married Sally
White, a cultured and handsome woman from Stamford, Connecticut.[4] Sally White soon joined her husband's Congregational church
and subsequently became active in a small society whose members
met to read the Bible and to fashion commentaries on the text. With
her forceful character, she exhibited a fighting spirit concerning her
husband's professional duties. She regarded Christian life as a "war-
fare" that has "powerful enemies to encounter from within and without."[5] She helped her husband by recording many passages in the
church records, and she also probably passed along her religious
devotion to her children.

By 1810, the year of Betsey Cowles's birth, Sally and the Reverend
Cowles enjoyed a sizable family of four sons and four daughters.
Edwin Weed, born in May 1794, was followed by Sally Berien on 21
February 1796; William Elbert on 5 January 1798; Edward Giles
Hooker on 26 September 1801; Martha Hooker on 13 May 1804;
the twins, Lysander Mix and Cornelia Rachel on 11 August 1807;
and Betsey Mix on 9 February 1810.[6] With such a large family to feed
and clothe, the Reverend Cowles pleaded with the Ecclesiastical
Council of Bristol to raise his salary, but the council persistently
declined any measures to increase the minister's income. Consequently, after his last daughter's birth in 1810, Cowles began to think
about finding a more lucrative means of support.[7]

To Cowles's surprise, the answer to his financial pinch came from
six hundred miles to the west. In the spring of 1810, a woman named
Sibbell Austin arrived in Bristol soliciting a minister for a small
Congregational church in Austinburg, Ohio.[8] Confronting the Reverend Cowles and his wife, Sibbell Austin explained that a pioneer band
of Congregationalists in the tiny Western Reserve community needed
a minister. They were willing to pay a decent salary and provide land
to an agreeable preacher. He would be paid two hundred dollars a
year by the Connecticut Missionary Society and an additional two
hundred dollars annually by the Austinburgers and would also re-
ceive eighty acres of land for a parsonage plus eighty acres for private

use.[9] Furthermore, he could purchase additional land at a comparatively low rate.

Austin's generous offer appealed to the Reverend Cowles. With his wife's encouragement he promptly introduced the idea to the Bristol Ecclesiastical Council. Although saddened by the loss of such an able and faithful minister, the council agreed to relieve Cowles of his Bristol ministry and free him to serve as a missionary in the Connecticut Western Reserve. After his formal dismissal and farewell sermon on 30 May 1810, the Reverend Cowles embarked alone on a preliminary missionary tour of the area before subjecting his young family to the long journey west.[10]

On the missionary tour Cowles saw for the first time the land known as the "Ohio Country," part of the vast Connecticut Western Reserve. The Reserve, formed in 1786, was settled after 1795 by a group of men later named the Connecticut Land Company. As one of the fifty-three subscribers, Sibbell Austin's husband, Judge Eliphalet Austin, helped to survey, partition, and prepare the land for settlers.[11] The small community of Austinburg thus received its name from the ambitious judge. By 1810, when the Reverend Cowles arrived, there were only ten families settled in the whole of Austinburg township. Among these pioneer families were the Mills, Cases, Wrights, Phelps, Cowles, Nettlesons, Hawleys, and Austins.[12]

The Reverend Cowles soon learned that the early Austinburgers had worked hard to build a successful community. Austinburg township was located on a partially cleared east-west road, traversed by the first party of surveyors in 1798. In 1800 the first town settlers cut a north-south road from Austinburg to the Ashtabula Creek, intersecting the original east-west route. The Austin road, later known as the "Salt Road" was subsequently extended southward through Morgan, New Lyme, Colebrook, and Wayne townships in Ashtabula County, and further to Kinsman and Poland, both in Trumbull County. An improved east-west route was soon established to Harpersfield and Jefferson townships. In addition to better transportation routes, by 1810 Austinburg had acquired a sawmill and a grist mill. Built by Judge Austin in 1801, the sawmill was situated at Mechanicsville in the extreme western section of the township and the grist mill was constructed nearby. Both of these convenient improvements were located on Grand River which flowed northward from Trumbull County, through Mechanicsville, then sharply turned westward, emptying into Lake Erie at Fairport.[13] In 1803, Ohio was admitted to the Union, and Ashtabula County received its boundaries in 1807.

The ten original town families founded the First Congregational Church of Austinburg—the first in the Western Reserve. The church group was served by the Reverend Joseph Badger, an itinerant minister for the Connecticut Missionary Society. The sixteen charter members of the church met alternately at Deacon Sterling Mills's cabin in the south end of the township and at Judge Austin's cabin in the north end. In 1803 a log meeting house was finally built at the geographical center of the township to accommodate the scattered town settlers.[14] The center church, the church Cowles was soon to inherit, was built of unhewn logs, two miles from any one settlement in the middle of a forest. At one end of the isolated church a wooden door swung on wooden hinges and at the other end a huge stick and mud chimney sufficed for heat and light. A window with eight to twelve glass panes graced each side wall. The floor was laid from smooth split logs, slabs served as benches, and the pulpit was a candle stand and a chair imported from the nearest dwelling. Since every family in Austinburg converged at the center church on the Sabbath, the Reverend Badger's decision to leave in 1809, greatly disturbed the community's only religious institution.[15]

In spite of the church's primitive structure and setting, the Reverend Cowles was decidedly impressed with the town's facilities and friendly population. He resolved to fill the vacant position at the Austinburg church, and to bring his family to the Western Reserve the following spring. Cowles finished his tour and in late September departed the Western Reserve. He arrived in Bristol in mid-October to find his wife and eight children in good health.[16]

During the following winter Cowles readied his family and possessions for the long journey west. As the time for the trip approached, old parishioners from Bristol, Farmington, and the surrounding area, flocked to the parsonage to wish Cowles and his family farewell. On 14 May 1811, the Reverend Cowles, his wife, eight children, and Mr. Sheperd, a hired man, departed Bristol for the famed "Ohio Country."[17] During their trek the family relied on two ox-drawn wagons to carry most of their household possessions and dozens of books. The minister, his wife, and the smaller children rode in a carriage. Since there would be few lodgings along the way, they brought two or three large trunks covered with deerskin to hold their bedding. Edwin, the eldest son was then seventeen years old; Sally, fifteen; William, thir-

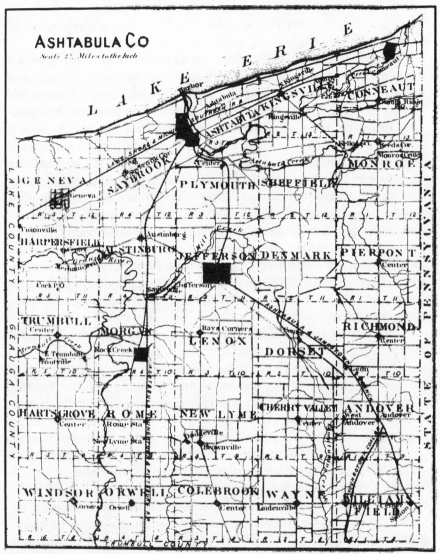

Townships of Ashtabula County, Ohio. Reproduced from Williams, *History of Ashtabula County, Ohio,* Philadelphia, 1878.

teen; Edward, ten; Martha, seven; Cornelia and Lysander, four; and the youngest, Betsey, was one year and three months of age.[18]

Although young Betsey Cowles remembered little or nothing about the family's westward trip, stories about the journey and similar treks in later years enhanced her appreciation for Ohio's early history and pioneer settlers. The Cowles family's journey was probably less difficult and safer than what would be expected for a family of ten crossing the forests, rivers, and mountains in the second decade of the nineteenth century. The party initially progressed fairly well, covering from twenty-five to thirty miles per day during pleasant, cool, and dry weather. The Reverend Cowles stopped on the Sabbath to sermonize to whomever would hear him and, except for Sally Cowles's extremely sore feet, the family maintained their health. The family bought provisions such as oats, corn, rye, bread, and bacon to eat along the way. Traveling the northern route through New York, Pennsylvania, and northern Ohio along the Lake Erie shore, they passed through many of the places that the Reverend Cowles had passed on his missionary tour the previous spring.

In the second week of the journey, it began to rain at intervals and the Cowles family was forced to unload part of their possessions and to pay for freightage. The carriage horse traveled less distance each day and lagged behind the wagons as much as seven miles at times.[19] A more serious and unexpected problem was the girls' deteriorating health. During the night of 29 May, after crossing a distance of thirty-four miles, the infant Betsey contracted a mysterious sickness. The next day, Sally fell ill after the party attempted to move on. With two sick children, the Reverend Cowles was forced to stop before noon in Geneva, New York, where he found a doctor and medicine for the children and the weary carriage horse also received attention. Betsey and Sally seemed improved the next day, so the party forged ahead twenty-nine miles to West Bloomfield, New York. On Saturday, 1 June, the family was forced to stop again in Avon because Betsey's condition worsened and Cornelia was also afflicted.

The family received shelter for the weekend in Avon, New York, where the Reverend Cowles preached to a considerable gathering, and by Monday morning the children were better. The family moved on, only to encounter more rain, swamps, mud, and rutted roads. One morning, on a particularly warped road, the larger wagon turned over and delayed the family yet another time. Thereafter the Cowles family progressed around twenty or fewer miles a day. By 13 June 1811, when the party reached Conneaut, Ohio, the children had fully recovered. The family arrived at Judge Austin's home late the next evening.[20]

When the Cowles family arrived in Austinburg, they stayed in the tiny log meeting house that was built in 1803. The meeting house was usually the temporary house of all new settlers in the community. The Reverend Cowles and helpful neighbors immediately commenced building a log cabin to house his family. By the fall of 1811, the Cowles family was comfortably situated in a cabin near the log meeting house. On 25 September 1811, the Reverend Cowles was installed as pastor of the First Congregational Church.[21]

In the following year the new minister decided that a New England-style frame church should replace the pioneer log meeting house. The leading townsmen, Judge Austin, Joab Austin, and Dr. Orestes K. Hawley agreed, and the four men raised enough local support to finance the project. Construction began immediately in the same vicinity as the old log dwelling, across from the Cowles's cabin. Although the men were content to build the church without a steeple, the women wanted one so strongly that several took in sewing and weaving to pay for one. Notably, the resulting steeple was the first erected on the Western Reserve. Although only partially finished, the frame church was pressed into use in 1815.[22]

While the frame church was still under construction, the Reverend Cowles started work on a parsonage to better accommodate his growing family. In the summer of 1812, Sally Cowles had given birth to a fifth son, Lewis, while the other children were quickly outgrowing the tiny log cabin. In the winter of 1813–14, the minister planned to build a large, Connecticut-style house directly opposite and west of the new church site. Actual construction was delayed because Mr. Sheperd, the hired man, drowned in Grand River attempting to transport logs for the structure to the Mechanicsville sawmill. The home was finally finished in 1815.[23]

This small Western Reserve community, its rugged, helpful inhabitants, the new church, the parsonage, and the winding river were among young Betsey Cowles's earliest memories of the "Ohio Country." She grew up an Ohioan with people who tried to build a comfortable home and social life out of a wilderness. Since her father was the town's minister, much of her early home and social life centered around religious events and church-related affairs. She and her brothers and sisters attended the Reverend Cowles's two Sunday

First Congregational Church of Austinburg, built, 1815. Reproduced from Williams, *History of Ashtabula County, Ohio,* Philadelphia, 1878.

Giles Hooker Cowles residence in Austinburg, built 1815. Reproduced from Williams, *History of Ashtabula County, Ohio.* Philadelphia, 1878.

services and his daily religious household gatherings. The Bible, their Savior, and the Congregational church were among the first things about which the young pioneer children learned and learned again.[24]

The community's big social event was quite often the "singing meeting." In Austinburg the singers rehearsed at the homes of Deacon Mills and Judge Austin or in the Cowles parsonage. After ample practice the members presented a "singing lecture" or concert to the local audience. Some of the minister's children, having inherited their mother's musical talent, sang regularly at the meetings. They became quite proficient at four-part harmony. Cornelia developed the greatest interest and talent for vocals and piano. She and Martha sang soprano; Betsey sang alto; and Lewis, tenor.[25]

Singing was only one favorite pastime for Betsey and Cornelia. They also enjoyed ice-skating, romping in the woods, and various other diversions. With only a few years difference between their ages, Betsey and Cornelia grew to be much alike, not only in appearance, but in opinion and disposition as well. Although Betsey was the thinner and more attractive, they were both healthy, sturdy-looking girls with thick brown hair, dark eyes, and fair complexions. Both were clever, witty, and bright. Betsey's sense of humor and playful disposition complemented Cornelia's aptitude for telling humorous stories and playing practical jokes. They grew to love the outdoors, big social events, and lively conversations. Betsey and Cornelia became the closest and dearest of sisters.

Educational opportunities were limited to the local, frontier facilities. There were no public schools in Austinburg, or anywhere in Ohio at that time, so education outside the home depended on local, private initiative.[26] In 1818, Deacon Moses Wilcox of the Austinburg Congregational Church began to teach a Sunday school which was probably limited in its curriculum to religious subjects. For the basics of reading, writing, and arithmetic, Austinburg youth could attend "subscription schools." These schools were usually conducted by a local or itinerant schoolmaster who arranged to have as many as twenty children come to class. The teacher received a modest stipend of $1.75 to $2.25 per student for one school term, usually about ten to twelve weeks. Teachers of such schools "boarded around," that is, they shifted from one student's home to another for a place to eat and sleep.[27]

For classes the schoolmaster and pupils would congregate in whatever structure was available. The pupils sat on benches fashioned from split logs with legs attached to the rounded underside.[28] Typically there were two school terms per year. A summer term ran approximately from June to August and a winter term ran from December to March. Since the teacher and parents arranged school terms, their months and duration varied locally according to how many pupils could be subscribed and how many were needed at home to help with fall harvest and spring planting.[29]

Girls who attended school regularly were frequently training to become teachers and Betsey Cowles, as well as some of her sisters, became interested in pursuing such a career. In 1823, at the age of sixteen, Cornelia Cowles ventured to Kinsman in Trumbull County to secure pupils for a winter term; and in 1826, Martha journeyed to her cousins' home in the Catskills of New York to gather a class.[30] In the following year the Reverend Cowles volunteered Betsey to substitute for the absent teacher in the "East road" schoolhouse. Accordingly, she repaired through the Austinburg woods to dispense lessons at the school. After one week the novice teacher refused to return to the school for a second week of classes. Cornelia, who had more experience, completed the term.[31]

As unpleasant as Betsey Cowles's first teaching experience was, its effect was brief. The next year, at age eighteen, she engaged to teach in a small school near Warren in Trumbull County and successfully completed the term.[32] She began to like teaching, even more than did her older sisters, and conducted many school terms in the Austinburg vicinity in the late 1820s and early 1830s. Through these years Cowles became extremely popular with the area youth while local parents recognized her unusual skill and talent for instructing children of all ages. Cowles regarded her pupils as friends, as well as young scholars, and they reflected their affection by familiarly addressing their mentor as "Aunt Betsey."[33] Throughout Cowles's subsequent long career in the field of education, the title was the one by which most students knew, addressed, and remembered their teacher.

In addition to teaching in the early 1830s, Cowles supported western educational growth through organized benevolence and was receptive to new ideas in the education field. She joined the Young Ladies Education Society of Austinburg, a local affiliate of the American Education Society. In 1833 and 1834 she served as secretary.[34] A new trend in the education field, to which she was particularly attracted, was the infant school techniques of Joanna Graham Bethune. Bethune's husband, Divie Bethune, helped to found the American

Bible Society, the New York Sunday School Union Society, and the New York Religious Tract Society. Widowed in the 1820s, Joanna Bethune carried on her husband's philanthropic work, devoting herself to instructing the very young. In 1827, she founded an infant school society in New York, and subsequently became superintendent of at least nine infant schools in the city. One of those was in the Five Points District, a notorious slum. Bethune's successes in New York and her books on infant education were responsible for popularizing infant school methods in the United States.[35]

Attracted by the new idea of teaching children between the ages of four and six years old, Cowles took time from her Austinburg classes to learn more about infant school methods. In the spring of 1832, she obtained a favorable letter of introduction to the teacher of an infant school in Kinsman, Ohio. Bethune served as the school's patroness. After the study and practice of infant school techniques in Kinsman, Cowles conducted several such schools there and in the Austinburg vicinity.[36] Cowles rendered her lessons with methods resembling later-day education techniques. For instance, teachers in infant schools taught multiplication tables with rhyming, rhythmic songs, and employed visual aids such as globes and dangling planetary systems to teach the basics of geography and astronomy.[37]

When the aspiring pedagogue was not in the classroom, she participated in the typical activities of frontier women such as the practical quilting and sewing bees, and the more intellectual literary society. In the spring of 1834, Betsey, Cornelia, and eleven other young Austinburg women, formed the Young Ladies Society for Intellectual Improvement. The group met every two weeks to discuss scientific, political, and domestic subjects, for the purpose of self-education. It required each member to propose discussion material and to submit ideas on adopted topics. In 1835, Cowles served as secretary of the society, which no doubt contributed to the early development of her intellectual interests and independent thinking.[38]

One of the organization's favorite discussion topics was the United States presidents from Washington to Jackson. Each president received a lengthy eulogy, although the women noted the "very offensive" sedition and alien laws passed during John Adams's administration and were dubious about Jackson's bank policy. One member, Sarah Austin, remarked that people might think it strange for young ladies to discuss such topics, but the group agreed that it was proper if they diffused their knowledge since an enlightened populace comprised the key to good democracy. Although the members did not mention formal female education in particular, they were convinced that God had formed their minds "capable of improvement" and that self-education increased their usefulness to others.[39]

The women expressed a particularly strong opinion concerning current regional events such as the influx of a Catholic element and slave colonization. Their anti-Catholic consensus was based on their belief that most "papists" were self-seeking money-mongers who only did good deeds to buy their friends out of purgatory. They anticipated that the Catholics would "get up an army" to take over the Mississippi Valley and other regions, and that Catholic schools would trap unsuspecting Protestant children. Their views on this subject were in harmony with prevailing Protestant fears at the time.[40]

The society's typical anti-Catholic prejudice was offset by its atypical approach to American slavery. The majority of the Western Reserve populace agreed that slavery was morally wrong, and pockets of Garrisonian immediate abolitionism existed in the area. Still, plans to cope with the problem such as colonization, gradual emancipation, or non-expansion were generally much more popular than immediate emancipation.[41] Even as late as 1837, when the national Colonization Society was effectively defunct, some Austinburgers remained supportive of the failing organization's area branch.[42] Other Austinburgers though, responded to the immediate abolitionist demands of a few Western Reserve ministers. Austinburgers formed the core of the all-male Ashtabula County Anti-Slavery Society organized in Ashtabula on 27 May 1834. As an auxiliary of the Western Reserve Anti-Slavery Society, at its first annual meeting on 4 July 1834, the Austinburg branch proposed the "speedy and utter extinction of slavery," denounced the Colonization Society, and resolved to petition Congress in favor of immediate abolition.[43]

The Austinburg young ladies, not permitted by custom to join the men's anti-slavery organization, were nevertheless interested in the issue. Within a few weeks after the men formed the county anti-slavery society, Cowles's group discussed slavery at one of its early meetings in June 1834. Probably influenced more by their local male counterparts than by direct exposure to Garrison's *Liberator,* the Austinburg women agreed that slavery was a moral issue and that colonizing free blacks had no tendency to diminish the number of slaves either directly or indirectly. Their conclusion, like William Lloyd Garrison's, was that "immediate emancipation of the slaves" was the duty of the

American people and that "moral influence on the slaveholder" was the best method to accomplish emancipation.[44]

Although these women, enjoying some local sympathy, were not alone in their anti-slavery sentiments, immediate abolitionists were generally an unpopular minority in the Reserve area at the time. Nevertheless, they were adamant in their belief that slavery was a moral wrong and should be corrected immediately and without compromise. As a society member and an officer, Betsey Cowles's early views on slavery were undoubtedly reflected in its moral discourse. The following year, she helped to form the Ashtabula County Female Anti-Slavery Society and, in 1835, served as its secretary.

While Cowles, and her sisters Cornelia and Martha to a lesser extent, were occupied with church affairs, local schools, and social organizations, some of the other Cowles children married and raised families of their own. The oldest brother, Edwin Weed, became a doctor under the tutelage of Dr. Orestes K. Hawley. In 1815, he married Almira Mills Foote. In 1819, Cowles's oldest sister Sally Berien, married Judge Austin's son, the Reverend Eliphalet Austin. William Elbert, who took up farming, married Lydia R. Wolcott in 1827. Each of these families had several children. The many young nephews and nieces were an important and welcomed addition to Betsey Cowles's life.

Tragedy also befell the Cowles family. In 1823, one of the older brothers, Edward Giles Hooker, died at age twenty-two. In 1830, Sally White Cowles died and, five years later, Giles Hooker.[45] Since most of the surviving family scattered to make their own homes and raise families, the three unmarried Cowles sisters, with the aid of Lysander and his wife Rachel, took charge of the family's property and house. Cornelia and Betsey Cowles inherited jointly one-third of the real estate value while Lysander received the other two-thirds.[46] Although not a legal property recipient, Martha actually took charge of the general domestic responsibilities of the household, while Betsey and Cornelia desired much more to travel and to generate independent means of support.

By the mid-1830s, at age twenty-six, Betsey Cowles had already expressed an interest in some of the concerns that later dominated her life. Although her initial teaching efforts were difficult and rather episodic, her growing popularity with students and townspeople, rendered the teaching profession a most attractive endeavor. She also participated in Austinburg's early benevolent social circles such as the local Education Society and the Young Ladies Society for Intellectual Improvement. For a female of her day, Cowles displayed an uncommon tendency toward self-reliance. The deaths of Cowles's parents only increased her initiative and independence. At a time when most young women focused their lives on attracting a husband, Cowles wished "there was no such thing as marrying."[47]

2
From Granville to Oberlin

FROM the mid-1830s to the mid-1840s, Betsey Cowles embraced two spheres of public activity—education and abolitionism—which were to occupy a large part of her working life. She continued to teach locally, but began to regard pedagogy as a lifetime occupation rather than as a prematrimonial pastime. She developed specific ideas concerning female education, personal independence, and self-reliance that surfaced early in her repudiation of marital ties and later in her pursuit of higher learning at Oberlin College. In the abolition sphere, Cowles took to heart the anti-slavery arguments of the Austinburg Female Intellectual Society. By helping to organize women's anti-slavery societies and by circulating petitions for the cause, Cowles became a leader of Ashtabula County's female anti-slavery sentiment.

To some degree, Cowles's anti-slavery views were an extension of broader convictions held in common with heirs of the New England concepts of organized benevolence. One of the most important and widespread religious concepts of the 1820s and 1830s, this tradition inspired organizations such as the American Education Society, the American Peace Society, and multiple temperance and anti-slavery groups.[1] As a member of the Austinburg Moral Reform Society, Cowles held at least a passive interest in a variety of reform causes in addition to abolitionism. By the mid-1830s, she earned the label "teetotal" on slavery as well as on temperance.[2]

Cowles's abolitionist views during the 1830s represented the generally unpopular minority fringe of anti-slavery sentiments on the Western Reserve. Although traditionally Reserve inhabitants opposed slavery, most were dubious about tampering with the institution for fear of southern unrest, interstate antagonism, or business ruptures. The Reserve populace in general was content to disapprove of the institution but, nevertheless, to tolerate it or endorse the ineffective Colonization Society. Indeed, in the 1830s, this view was generally prevalent in the entire state of Ohio.[3] However, a minority of anti-slavery advocates were not content to tolerate American slavery. They wanted to abolish it either gradually or immediately. This minority was extremely unpopular but it had spokesmen in Ohio as early as 1817, when Charles Osborn published the *Philanthropist* advocating immediate emancipation. In 1821, Benjamin Lundy started his gradualist paper, *The Genius of Universal Emancipation*.[4] Most notable, in the early 1830s, a small abolitionist circle whose members hailed largely from Yale or the Oneida Institute, lodged as faculty or students at Western Reserve College in Hudson, Ohio.[5]

These frail voices of abolitionism were strengthened by the impracticality of colonization efforts. The Western Reserve branches of the American Colonization Society had received ample vocal endorsement by Ohio newspapers and college students in the late 1820s, but financial support and enthusiasm for the cause were lacking. When the Negro population in southern Ohio increased while the Colonization Society coffers decreased, the question of contending permanently with black migrants came to strong light. Consequently, many colonizationists turned to supporting Ohio Black Laws, intended to discourage blacks from entering the state. Others rallied to either the gradual or immediate abolition cause.[6]

The effects of eastern organizational developments, however, bolstered Ohio abolitionist ranks. In 1833, the American Anti-Slavery Society (AASS) was founded in Philadelphia. Soon after, it began to sponsor Ohio agents in order to convert the population to abolitionism and to form auxiliary societies. Garrison's Boston *Liberator* was slowly gaining a readership with the financial aid of New Yorker Arthur Tappan and other eastern benefactors. In addition, as early as 1831 Theodore Weld had traversed parts of Ohio spreading the gospel of immediate emancipation, most notably at Lane Seminary in Cincinnati.[7] Weld so thoroughly convinced some of the Lane seminarians to embrace abolitionism that, in 1834, he and the converts defended their rights of free speech on the issue. Rather than compromise their principles, a substantial number of seminarians defied school trustees and transferred to Oberlin College which subsequently became a fortress of Reserve abolitionism.[8] In 1835, the AASS reported 328 new affiliated societies, one of which was the Ohio Anti-Slavery Society.[9] In the same year, the latter organization announced that the number of its auxiliary societies had risen from twenty to one hundred and twenty, claiming approximately 10,000 members.[10] In short, the early 1830s were years of organizational growth and expansion for both eastern and western abolitionists. At

Betsey Mix Cowles, ca. 1830s. ". . . made for more than to flutter or to serve." Betsey Mix Cowles Papers. Courtesy of the American History Research Center, Kent State University Libraries.

the grassroots level, Cowles exemplified an early practitioner of the emancipation creed which helped to muster the region's anti-slavery sentiments, producing such increases in membership.

Cowles's contribution to the anti-slavery cause came before the 1836 anniversary of the Ohio Anti-Slavery Society (OASS) at Granville, Ohio. The general purpose of the OASS entailed drumming up support, organizing societies, collecting contributions, formulating resolutions, and circulating petitions to abolish the slave trade in the District of Columbia.[11] In these endeavors the OASS was particularly inspired by Theodore Weld and the national group. At that time the AASS adhered to Garrison's Declaration of Sentiments adopted in 1833. The object of the AASS and its affiliates was to abolish entirely and immediately slavery in the United States by appealing to the moral consciences of fellow citizens. To this end, the society's constitution stated that its members would "endeavor in a constitutional way to influence Congress to put an end to the domestic slaver-trade, and to abolish slavery in all those portions of our common country, which come under its control, especially in the District of Columbia. . . ."[12] The national society then set the wheels in motion for a vast petition campaign enlisting the aid of state and local groups. Simultaneously, it labored to convince fellow citizens, "by arguments addressed to their understanding and consciences, that slaveholding is a heinous crime in the sight of God, and that the duty, safety, and best interests of all concerned, require its immediate abandonment, without expatriation."[13]

Undoubtedly, Betsey Cowles along with her sisters, Martha and Cornelia, and other members of the Austinburg Ladies Society for Intellectual Improvement, agreed wholeheartedly with these contentions. Although Ashtabula County had had an anti-slavery society as early as 1834, it was weak, inactive, and exclusively male.[14] Females typically formed their own groups for the cause in accord with social propriety, although mixed groups were not unprecedented. Shortly after the Ohio Anti-Slavery Society congealed in 1835, Cowles spearheaded a movement to organize the Ashtabula County anti-slavery women into a female auxiliary organization. At least nine of the original thirteen members of the Austinburg Ladies Society for Intellectual Improvement joined the new anti-slavery group for females.[15] Austinburger Lovina Bissel served as the first president; Mrs. Dr. Hawley as vice-president; and Cowles as corresponding secretary.

The main task of the Ashtabula County Female Anti-Slavery Society was to gather small existing female groups under one county banner. The members also wanted to initiate new societies, and to provide the necessary moral suasion to attract new members. As the corresponding secretary, Cowles urged the formation of township ladies societies, monitored their progress, and at times secured suitable speakers for their meetings.[16] She also circulated an immediate emancipation petition for presentation at the OASS anniversary in Granville on 27 and 28 April 1836.

Cowles's efforts met with typical opposition in many of the Ashtabula County townships. For example, Rachel Babcock of Wayne township thanked Cowles for sending an organizing agent but reported that prospects were not favorable. Most of the Wayne women were "in doubt whether it is suitable for Ladies to go forward in so publick [sic] a cause. . . ."[17] From Andover township Sarah Coleman reported a newly found society of thirty-eight members. She added that husbands who "try to make them believe there is hypocrisy in it" prevented many other women from joining.[18] Opposition of a different nature came from Rome and New Lyme townships. Joanna Chester stated that Rome's society was floundering because local people who opposed slavery did not approve of the group's abolitionist solution.[19] L. Arnold of New Lyme contended with a similar problem. She did not dare circulate Cowles's petition since New Lymers would rather colonize slaves.[20] Jefferson's society allowed women to join, thus rendering an exclusively female organization undesirable.[21]

As discouraging as this may have been, Cowles's family and local anti-slavery activists encouraged her to solicit female support for the unpopular cause. All of Cowles's brothers and sisters were staunch abolitionists as were many of the leading townspeople. Members of the state society also voiced their approval of Cowles's efforts. Although A. A. Guthrie of the OASS warned Cowles about strong, statewide opposition, he also emphasized that women were particularly capable of exerting moral suasion and that it was their "most appropriate duty to be zealously and constantly engaged in pleading the cause of abolition."[22] Another OASS spokesman and former Lane seminarian, Augustus Wattles, reiterated Guthrie's theme. He reminded Cowles that women could properly step out of their usual sphere in the case of abolition work. " 'In Jesus Christ,' " he quoted, " 'there is neither male nor female,' " and continued, "that is in moral enterprises, moral worth and intellect are the standards. A mind whether deposited in a male or a female body is equally valuable for all moral and intellectual purposes."[23] Going beyond the advocacy of equality in reform, Wattles suggested a radical departure from the contemporary concept of separate spheres for women and men. "Indeed there is no station in life but what may be filled as ably and beneficially by woman as by man," he contended, "the difference is made principally by education. Abolition is opening a new field for female effort."[24] Wattles also urged Cowles to arrange for the appointment of female delegates to the approaching Granville anniversary.

Although Cowles certainly agreed with Guthrie and Wattles's opinions, she hardly needed convincing. Her initial effort to organize Ashtabula County women came prior to their encouragement. However, their comments concerning women's intellectual potential probably served to reinforce her opinion on the subject. As to women in the anti-slavery field, even the secretary of the large Portage County Female Anti-Slavery Society recognized Cowles's enthusiasm and looked to her for advice. The Portage secretary observed, "Many curl the lip, and cast the look of scorn when women associate their efforts in the cause. They fear the strength that union gives so they cry, out of your sphere ladies, you have forgotten that modesty and retirement belonging to your sex."[25]

For unknown reasons Cowles did not attend the Granville meeting, but her absence from the affair was not because women were excluded. Of the 192 delegates nearly two dozen were females. Nor was it because she did not have proper company for the journey, since three Austinburgers represented Ashtabula County at the gathering and Cowles could have easily accompanied them. Furthermore, attending notables such as A. A. Guthrie, Augustus Wattles, and the Reverend Henry Cowles of Oberlin, as well as brother Lysander would have welcomed her presence. Perhaps occupied with the school term, Cowles did not venture to Granville, but the results of her previous year's labor were officially recorded in the OASS's list of affiliate societies. Of the twelve female groups reporting to the Granville meeting, the Ashtabula County Female Society was the largest organization with 437 members. The next largest women's society was the Portage County organization with 300 members. Moreover, Cowles's group was the second largest anti-slavery society in the entire state, second only to the 942-member Paint Valley Society of Portage

County which was not exclusively female.[26] After the meeting one participant commented that in spite of "considerable prejudice against ladies county soc[ieties]," Cowles's group produced a "mighty change in the public sentiment" in the Ashtabula region.[27] Thus, Cowles entered the abolition field with unusually impressive results.

In addition to her abolition work, Cowles developed a deepening interest in education. As a result of her intermittent engagements at local schools, she began to contemplate education's nature, meaning, and uses. For Cowles, education represented a religious enterprise which fulfilled God's plan for rational creatures. Those with rational faculties were obliged to cultivate their gift. In an 1835 essay entitled, "A Good Scholar," authored while teaching Austinburg girls, she noted,

> Every object of nature affords a subject for profitable study; the mind is so formed; that it can contemplate these objects not only with pleasure, but with profit. God hath created all, with the evident design, that his rational creatures; should improve every faculty; in contemplating his character, as exhibited in his works of creation. Those who neglect the improvement of these faculties, bury the talents which God hath given and thus abuse his rich blessing.[28]

Applying these beliefs to the real world meant elevating the standard of education in general and of female education in particular. However, opportunities for such labor were limited in Austinburg and Cowles's best efforts to realize this ambition did not come until after the completion of her formal education at Oberlin College.

In the 1830s, Cowles's pedagogy was scattered, irregular, and interrupted by domestic affairs, as well as by interstate travel.[29] Although both Cornelia and Betsey inherited jointly $2,000 worth of the family's real estate, neither sister cared to sacrifice ambition for domestic bliss. Martha, who was more of a homebody, accepted the farm's responsibilities with the help of brothers Lewis, Lysander, and William Cowles.

Cornelia Cowles worked as a professional musician. In 1837, she performed in the Reverend Aiken's church in Cleveland and in the following year she traveled to Brooklyn, New York, where she sang at St. Peter's Episcopal Church.[30] She earned quite a reputation in the Cleveland area for several "conspicuous" parts in public concerts.[31] When at home Cornelia sang with Betsey and Lewis at local anti-slavery and religious gatherings. Some townspeople even regarded the family trio's talent as equal to that of the famous Hutchinson Family singers.[32]

In addition to vocalizing, Cornelia studied piano, most notably with a group of Detroit Catholic nuns in 1836. Thereafter she periodically taught and studied both the keyboard and voice. Lessons from Catholic nuns did not bother lighthearted Cornelia in the least, but her younger sister worried about the musician "lest she should be made a papist."[33] Dr. Harry Wadsworth, the Reverend Cowles's grand-nephew, reassured Betsey that Cornelia was as "strongly predisposed to see the devil's cloven hoof in everything connected with popery as even you could wish. . . ."[34]

While the Cowles sister's opposition to Catholicism was unwavering, their commitment to the family's Congregational faith was variable. They were quite liberal-minded with respect to Protestantism and were tempted to dabble in other Protestant faiths during their early excursions from Austinburg. From January to September 1837, Cowles taught in the New York Catskills where her cousins, the Roots, resided. There she was strongly drawn to the revivalistic, freewilling Methodist ranks. In the same year, Cornelia was attracted to the Baptist faith while singing for a Baptist church in Cleveland. Learning of their mutual religious deviations, Cornelia told her younger sister, "If you should become a methodist and I a baptist I don't know what would be done however if we are good girls I don't think any one would ask what we were."[35] Adding a tongue-in-cheek comment addressed to the Roots concerning her younger sister's past behavior, Cornelia stated, ". . . [I] am glad if you think Betsey is of any kind of use or does good anywhere, hope you will take care of her, keep her straight and I hope your Methodist brethren will in the end make something of her, for we have been obliged to give it up some time ago."[36] Whether Cornelia officially embraced the Baptist faith is unknown, but Betsey most certainly professed Methodism at least while she taught in the Catskills.[37]

Cowles carried the abolitionists's creed and her moral reform enthusiasm to the Catskills, making quite an impression upon her relatives and acquaintances. She made sure her cousins received the *Emancipator,* organ of the AASS, during and after her visit. Boldly, she also circulated copies of the *Advocate of Moral Reform,* an unusually lurid sheet designed to unveil the evils lurking for young unguarded women. It operated under the motto: "For there is nothing covered that shall not be revealed; neither hid that shall not be made known."[38] The Roots's reaction to Cowles's mini-crusade was varied. She successfully converted them to abolitionism, but shocked them by peddling the provocative *Advocate*. After Cowles returned to Austinburg, Antoinette, one of her Catskill cousins wrote, "Betsey I have not heard a word in favor of slavery since you left. It is known that we or you are abolitionists where ever we are known, for everyone I have seen since you left have something to say about it, but we poor dunces can say nothing at . . . all."[39] She mentioned further that the local Methodist ministers passed a resolution forbidding abolitionist discussions and consequently wanted her undaunted cousin Cowles to send abolition literature. The *Advocate*, however, did not gain much popularity. Maria Palen refused to take the *Advocate* from the post office after the Ohioan's departure because she regarded it as a "dirtisome" paper and it was a "disgrace to be seen with one." Catherine Root vowed to burn every one of the papers she saw.[40]

After Cowles passed the age of twenty-five, her friends in the Catskills and in Austinburg predicted that the aspiring teacher would soon marry. In 1835, Matilda Howell, one of Cowles's dearest home-town friends, predicted that Cowles would be "a worshiper at the shrine of Hymen" within the year."[41] But two years later she was still single at the age of twenty-seven. Consequently, Cornelia highly recommended a Reverend Mr. Sanders as a "good good man . . . plain in appearance," and the recipient of a lot and a house if he married in the near future. "Unless you make up your mind to lead a life of single blessedness," husband-hunting Cornelia advised, "don't you refuse Brother S[anders]. . . ."[42] Dr. Theodore Harry Wadsworth who joined the family circle in 1836, represented another romantic prospect. Wadsworth, a native of Farmington, Connecticut, and only two years younger than Cowles, was her father's grand-nephew and an educated, dedicated, witty, and mystical physician.[43] Playing cupid again, Howell sent Cowles the following message: ". . . you will find the end of a string . . . in a letter, wh[ich] will unite you & this Harry in the bonds of matrimony, being fastened to him in Austinburg & you in Catskill."[44] On the other hand, the aged Sibbell Austin advised Cowles not to marry until she was forty years old, but instead to spend her time teaching and "doing good." "If you marry now," Austin cautioned, "you will not be as happy as you are single." But old Mrs. Austin, Howell interjected, gave that advice to everyone.[45]

In spite of several matrimonial prospects Cowles was content to remain single. In 1837, Cowles reiterated her view that she did not know or care anything about marriage and by the spring of 1838, although rumors persisted, she had convinced nearly everyone that she truly was not interested in marriage.[46]

Cowles's marital apprehensions may have been due to her overriding desire for further education at Oberlin College. The Cowles family had taken an interest in the school since its founding in 1833. Austinburg's Congregational minister, the Reverend Henry Cowles, moved to Oberlin as Professor of Languages and his wife, Alice Welch Cowles, followed as Principal of the Female Department.[47] Their daughter Rachel married Cornelia's twin brother Lysander and lived at the Austinburg homestead. Lysander and Lewis were among Oberlin's first students in 1835 and 1836. Lewis was quite satisfied with the school's manual labor system and its faculty, especially abolitionist President Asa Mahan. Lysander represented Oberlin as one of the anti-slavery Granville delegates.[48] Although one of Oberlin's singular features was its abolitionist atmosphere, most notably for the Cowles sisters, the institution opened its doors to women.

Ironically, enrolling in the Oberlin Ladies Course was not Cowles's original idea. In 1837 hats and fancy fashions for a trip to New York City were of more interest to the young teacher than renewing her education in faraway Lorain County, Ohio.[49] The original idea belonged to Rachel Cowles who tried to convince not Betsey, but her older sister Martha that she should enroll at Oberlin. In the summer of 1837, Martha requested her younger sister's advice on the proposition. Most probably any advice given was negative since the request implied that if Martha should go to Oberlin, either Betsey or Cornelia would have to take over the domestic duties.[50] The idea appealed to Betsey more for its application to her, the aspiring teacher, than for its application to Martha. Consequently, when Cowles returned to Austinburg in the fall of 1837, she carried with her the idea of attending Oberlin.[51] Rationalizing, she told Cornelia, "Martha will feel lonely to have us both gone but she is not so dependent as we are for society. . . ."[52] Martha evidently lost interest in the prospect, but Betsey applied for entry into the Ladies Course, and in August 1838, she learned of her acceptance.

A Congregational institution, Oberlin Collegiate Institute was dedicated to bringing a liberal arts education within the reach of all and to imparting the obligations of a Christian life to every student. Its first circular stated that the grand objects of the Oberlin Institute "are, to give the most useful education at the least expense of health, time, and money; and to extend the benefit of such education to both sexes and to all classes of the community, as far as its means will allow."[53] As president of Oberlin College, the abolitionist and former Lane Seminary trustee, Asa Mahan guided the student body, which included several Negroes. Between the Preparatory, Collegiate, Theological, and Female Departments, approximately four hundred students attended the booming institution.[54] With the school's manual labor system students could defray the cost of their education by working for part of their tuition and board. The school's expenses were funded largely by the well-known eastern philanthropists, Arthur and Lewis Tappan.

The Ladies Course at Oberlin was based on a four-year common-school education offering thorough training in mathematics, natural science, English literature, history, and philosophy. Language was confined to New Testament Greek and linear drawing constituted the only ornamental branch available to females. Generally, women in the Female Department's Ladies Course and men in the College Department's College Course attended the same classes. The arrangement tended to bring the two courses into harmony in fact, if not in name. Notably, in 1837, four women succeeded in gaining acceptance into the College Course. In 1841 three of the women received the first liberal arts degrees granted to women in the United States. In terms of labor, female students did much of the washing, ironing, and sewing for the other students in accord with the manual labor plan.[55] Academically though, the institution's objective concerning women was to "bring within the reach of the misjudged and neglected sex, all the instructive privileges which hitherto have unreasonably distinguished the leading sex from theirs."[56]

At Oberlin Cowles boarded with the Reverend Henry Cowles and his wife Alice Welch. Alice Welch Cowles led Oberlin's moral reformers as the first president of the Oberlin Female Moral Reform Society. The members supported and avidly read the *Advocate of Moral Reform*—the same publication with which Cowles shocked her Catskill cousins in 1837. In addition to promoting the *Advocate*, the professor's wife instructed Oberlin women to wear modest clothing and to shun public speaking.[57] Such a woman no doubt helped to modify temporarily her Austinburg boarder's worldly ways and diversion from the Congregational church. The professor's wife, Cowles stated, ". . . is all that a mother could be to me; in every point; I have never proved any individual to be so truly a friend as she has ever [been] to me and one most prominent evidence of her friendship is her willingness to tell me of my defects."[58] Cowles's defects, as she admitted, were that she, like her singing sister, was "more ready to yield to temptation than to resist."[59] She told Cornelia, "I cannot but think of the unnecessary care and trouble I have had and still have about myself (that is temporal concerns). I think if I can arrive at this point; feel perfectly willing that the Lord should take care of me; and trust him for it, it will certainly be a great relief. . . ."[60]

Although she was enrolled in the abbreviated Ladies Course, the full College Course vastly impressed Cowles as a means of elevating the female character. After a month at the school she reported to Cornelia,

> I do enjoy myself very much here; have not seen one thing upon which to fix that I dislike; everything is perfectly reasonable and rational, and everyone seems to be happy. The course of instruction is thorough; and so far as I can judge I must give this place the preference for Sarah & Charlotte [Austin] because it is the only place where females are conducted through a *full* and thorough course and it is this discipline that will truly elevate; for that reason I do want much that females should have it; their minds ought to be thus disciplined; and then they will become elevated.[61]

So impressed was Cowles with Oberlin's promise of elevating the female character through education that during her Oberlin years she become a rather informal, on-the-side recruiter for the Female Department. By October 1838, Cowles had already engaged a place for her niece, Sarah Austin, and intended for her to stay at least two or three years. Cowles wanted both Sarah and Charlotte Austin to complete the full female course and as many more as she could influence, especially the Catskillians. "If I was to come to Catskill," Cowles predicted, "I would try to raise a fever among some of the girls that my eye is upon. I mean a studying fever."[62]

After a year at Oberlin, Cowles's enthusiasm for female education intensified and subquently fancy-free Cornelia was the object of Cowles's criticism. "[I]f I was younger . . .," she began, "I would stay [at Oberlin] five years at least," and continued,

> Cornelia, I think it most lamentable that your mind is not disciplined by study; because nature has endowed you with abilities enough; & had they been improved as they should be; you would be far happier and better.

You would although you may laugh at me; & what is of far more weight in the scale, you might have done much . . . towards elevating the female character. Now it is true that woman in point of intellect does not occupy the station which was designed by her maker; & she never will until the standard of female education is elevated.

She concluded, "Oh! I do hope the time is not far distant when females will feel and act that they are made for something more than to flutter or to serve."[63] By the fall of 1839, Cowles firmly believed that women ought to have an education equal to that of men, and consequently the generalized system of female education needed thorough reform. "Your views respecting the meagreness of female education corresponds [sic] with my own," a Hudson student informed Cowles, "Reform is needed in this, as much as in many other things which are enlisting benevolent effort. I have strong hopes that you will do *much* towards effecting a change."[64]

Cowles excelled academically at Oberlin and also became popular socially among a close circle of Oberlinians. Some became notable figures in the institution's history. Among these were James Harris Fairchild, who became president of the college in 1866; Mary Ann Adams, Alice Welch Cowles's successor in 1839; and Horace C. Taylor, a Hudson transfer, first editor of the Oberlin *Evangelist*, and later a discredited thief.[65] Cowles's closest acquaintances, however, were dark, curly-headed Timothy B. Hudson and his future wife, Betsey Branch. Hudson, also a Western Reserve transfer, came to Oberlin in 1835, as a Latin tudor and served as professor of Latin and Greek from 1838 to 1841. He then temporarily resigned his position to Fairchild in order to travel as an abolition lecturer. He resumed his former professorial post in 1847, only to die in a tragic railroad accident in 1858.[66]

In the early 1840s, Hudson remarked that from the first time he saw dark-headed, smiling Cowles he marked her for a future friend. Indeed, the Oberlinians became remarkably close, partly as a result of the Austinburger's sisterlike guardianship to the "unknown [and] unattractive" Betsey Branch who was befriended, and finally drawn out of her "circle confined" by Cowles's outgoing personality.[67] As an anti-slavery lecturer in 1844, Hudson puzzled over how Cowles and he became such devoted friends considering their opposite personality traits. In a comparison very descriptive of his friend's nature, he pointed out to her, "My spirit is so stern, yours so playful. My character is so formal, yours so elastic & natural. My ways are so pedantic & magisterial, your manner [and] taste so entirely the reverse—My perceptions of the agreeable in social life so faulty— yours so delicate & true—that it is strange enough that you should have taken pleasure in my society."[68] Hudson married Branch on 8 December 1841, but Cowles's spirited influence over his new wife continued, leading to antagonism between herself and Hudson, who preferred domesticated women.[69]

Nevertheless, during Cowles's collegiate years she supported Hudson even through his several scandalous adventures. In 1840, for example, Hudson and a fellow Oberlinian were discovered attending a theatrical performance while at a college teachers' meeting in Columbus. Humiliated, the transgressors resigned, but were reinstated after considerable retribution. Even more shocking was Hudson's leadership in what commonly became known as the Norton Affair or the Oberlin Lynching. In July, 1840, Hudson and H. C. Taylor learned that one of the female students had received suggestive letters from Horace Norton, a preparatory student. Taylor subsequently intercepted a Norton letter that proposed a provocative woodland meeting. When Norton arrived at the proposed rendezvous expecting to find the young lady, he met instead the wrathful piety of fifteen Oberlin males led by Timothy Hudson. Failing to extract a confession by conventional prayer, the conspirators bared Norton's back and inflicted twenty-five lashes. Norton filed for damages and the case was so widely publicized that it marred the entire college's public image. Among those who excused Hudson and the others' lynch-law tactics were President Asa Mahan, the Reverend Henry Cowles, James Harris Fairchild, and Betsey Cowles.[70]

At Oberlin Cowles persisted in her Garrisonian abolitionism. When the American Anti-Slavery Society split in 1840, she was one of the very few Oberlinians who backed the Garrisonian faction, probably because of its emphasis on moral rather than political abolitionism and its allowing women to fully participate in societal endeavors. The great majority of Oberlin students and faculty, including Hudson, backed the rival American and Foreign Anti-Slavery Society, probably because the Tappans, important Oberlin benefactors, were anti-Garrisonian.[71] Due partly to Oberlin's anti-Garrisonian majority and partly to the pressures of academic obligations, Cowles's abolitionism was rendered essentially latent compared to what it had been between 1835 and 1837. Consequently, her active, public service for the cause did not reemerge under the Garrisonian banner until the mid-1840s.

After Cowles successfully completed two years in the Ladies Course in 1840, she planned to continue in Oberlin's full College Course. However, family finances were low in the wake of the 1837 economic slump. Cornelia, marooned in the Catskills, resorted reluctantly to pedagogy in order to earn enough money to proceed home. For Cowles, giving up the idea of returning to Oberlin was "quite a sacrifice," but since the circumstances called for additional income rather than expense, she sought a well-paying teaching position. In the spring of 1840, she received an offer in Michigan but a mix-up in plans caused her to lose it. Consequently, she was forced to wait in Austinburg for another offer.[72] She occupied the time with friends and family, spending part of the summer in Oberlin, the winter with Betsey Branch, and the following spring ministering to her seriously ill nephew, Giles Hooker Cowles, in Cleveland. Then she was summoned back to Austinburg to care for Lewis's wife, Claramond, who subsequently died in September 1841.[73]

Despite such varied domestic obligations, Cowles still hoped to secure a teaching position as soon as possible. In the quest she might never have traveled far from Austinburg had it not been for the assistance of a gentleman by the name of Lindsly who boarded at the Cowles homestead during the summer of 1841.[74] When Cowles learned that she might be able to secure a school in Magnolia or Leesville, Ohio, Lindsly offered to accompany her, thus facilitating her subsequent fifteen-week job search. In September 1841, the two pilgrims traveled to the small town of Magnolia, approximately ninety miles southwest of Austinburg. Barely a week away from home, Cowles found herself employed as a substitute store clerk in Magnolia while the Leesville folks invited her to start a female school and stay for a considerable period. She had little trouble making friends with her honest face, bubbling enthusiasm, and talent for sparking a conversation.

However, Cowles was optimistic that a better prospect could be found with persistent searching, so she opted to continue her much enjoyed trek with Lindsly.[75] A month later in Marietta, on the Ohio River, Cowles faced a "great dilemma." She wanted to "get permanently settled" with a school reasonably near home and did not want to remain idle all winter. The problem was that if she wanted work, her only prospect was in the distant state of Alabama. She might go home for the winter and wait for something in Ohio, but she was determined to teach as soon as possible.[76]

Since Cowles relished the independence and self-sufficiency of the prolonged excursion, the southern state's distance from home did not particularly weaken her resolution to work. Lindsly though solved the problem quickly by declining to escort his companion to Alabama. Since he planned to travel extensively in southern Ohio that winter, he promised to inquire further about schools and assured Cowles that she would eventually find academic employment. With this assurance, Cowles decided to winter in McConnelsville, Ohio, where possibilities seemed better. True to his word, Lindsly soon secured her an interview with the Reverend Mr. A. Williams, a Presbyterian minister who planned to establish a Portsmouth Seminary for young ladies.[77]

As a result of the interview, on 1 January 1842, Cowles received her first professional instructorship with the new Portsmouth Female Seminary. Williams acted as superintendent and Cowles as his assistant. Her starting salary was less than $25.00 a month for teaching about twenty-five young scholars. She fared well at the new school and Williams offered to raise her salary if she stayed at least another year.[78]

As much as Cowles liked the seminary, its location in Scioto County was not in Yankee country—a fact which thoroughly disgruntled her well-meaning friends and relatives. They would have preferred that she settle farther north and, consequently, bombarded her with letters with advice to leave the southern county. The Lorenzo M. Whiting family of Canton was particularly persistent in trying to pry Cowles away from Portsmouth. Whiting, a prominent, six-foot tall physician with a wry wit and a curious sociable nature, was a devoted friend to the Cowles sisters.[79] He collaborated with Cornelia in secretly promising Cowles's services to a Canton school, while she remained committed to Williams's seminary.[80] She probably would have taken the Canton offer after a summer visit with the Whitings, but since Williams expected her back in Portsmouth for the fall term, she regretted the "fix" and returned to Portsmouth. She told the disappointed Whitings, ". . . what is past is past; regrets are useless & what can't be cured must be endured; & I find it the best way to endure cheerfully."[81]

With her optimistic disposition, Cowles commenced the fall term of

1842 with high hopes. Having twenty-eight pupils she reported, "I am so busy that I have no time to be lonely, homesick or any thing of the kind; and my triafications [sic] during vacation; has given a double zest to my love of pedagoguering & I enter it with more ardor & pleasure; than ever before."[82] Sincerely enthusiastic and acting upon the principle, never too old to learn, she began taking drawing lessons, and planned to acquaint herself with all the fine arts. In addition to working on this ambition, she boldly assembled a Sabbath school admitting black children and consequently angered some Portsmouth whites. She revealed her non-racist attitude in the following explanation of the Sabbath school.

> I have been out & collected a class for myself in Sabbath School; ten girls; & they are guilty of the crime; what thinkeye it is? why of possessing real black skins; & for this crime, have been excluded from Sabbath school. Today one of them told me she liked much to come, but did not know she could for some of the white children were a going to leave, because they were there. I told her no: Sabbath schools were as much for black as for white; & if the white children left; we would have the house to ourselves.[83]

Subsequently, the white children withdrew from the school, but Cowles continued the Sabbath project as an educational and religious service for black youngsters. The black Sabbath school even continued under a different instructor after Cowles's departure from Portsmouth in the spring of 1843.[84]

As much as Cowles liked the Portsmouth seminary, she chose to leave for probably one overriding reason. She was not the type to cast roots, especially as far south as Scioto County. Her appetite for change and adventure had been whetted in the Catskills, at Oberlin, and during her travels with Lindsly. When in the spring of 1843, Gideon J. Leet, a Portsmouth public school official, offered to secure a "first rate school"[85] for Cowles in his district, she declined.

The Portsmouth Sabbath school situation exemplified Cowles's growing ability to take unpopular stands, such as abolitionism, without significantly marring her professional credibility. Her congenial personality enabled her peers to excuse her unpopular views in light of her professional talents. Cowles functioned academically almost oblivious to peer pressure or prevailing public opinion and retained the professional respect of her associates. Most notably, she did so as a

Garrisonian at Oberlin. Also she did not yield to Portsmouth whites on the Sabbath school issue. As a novice professional resolved to lead an independent life, Cowles's ability to command professional respect without compromising her principles was one of her most valuable personal assets.

3

The Grand River Institute and Abolitionism

LORENZO M. Whiting, who again arranged for Betsey Cowles to teach in Canton, was disappointed to learn that she was instead, "fitting young men and women for the ministry up there on the Presarve [sic]. . . ."[1] In the fall of 1843, the Canton physician reluctantly congratulated Cowles for having secured a new and prestigious teaching position with Austinburg's Grand River Institute (G.R.I.). Her unprecedented appointment as the first female principal of the G.R.I. Women's Department offered her an initial opportunity to implement the reforms in female education that she had envisioned since her Oberlin years. The institute's location allowed Cowles to live at home and thus to participate with anti-slavery groups to a much greater extent than when she had lived in Portsmouth. As a result, her G.R.I. years, from 1843 to 1848, were her most active in abolitionism.

Cowles's new school typified the frontier phenomenon of founding educational institutions. Unable to send their children East for higher education, the western members of various religious denominations founded multiple educational facilities between 1830 and 1860. With their tradition of an educated ministry from Harvard, Yale, and Dartmouth—western Congregationalists were particularly prone to establish local, church-sponsored schools. Cincinnati's Lane Theological Seminary and Oberlin's Theological Seminary, both founded in the 1830s, were two such Congregational-sponsored facilities in Ohio.[2]

Grand River Institute, like many other church-related preparatory schools, relied on local support and private endowments for its maintenance. The institute originated in 1831, when ten of Austinburg's Congregational leaders, among them the Reverend Giles Hooker Cowles, Dr. Orestes K. Hawley, and Judge Eliphalet Austin, obtained a state charter incorporating a school. It was initially intended to

46

prepare young men for the ministry.[3] Originally named the Ashtabula County Institute of Science and Industry, the Grand River Institute was established first in Mechanicsville on the Grand River since Hawley and Joab Austin had endowed the facility with the use of their property and mills near the river. The incorporators planned to allow students to work on the endowed land and at the various mills according to the manual labor system. The plan proved inadequate financially and was eventually abandoned. With these humble but promising foundations, Lucius M. Austin, the school's only instructor, taught science and mathematics to a handful of students.[4]

In 1836, the new school underwent several significant changes which led eventually to Cowles's appointment as principal of the Women's Department. In that year, enrollment increased substantially. Approximately thirty students, recruited by former Austinburger Henry Cowles, transfered to G.R.I. from overcrowded Oberlin. Likewise, the curriculum widened to include Latin and Greek, taught by Ralph M. Walker, the principal, with the temporary aid of Oberlin's Timothy Hudson. The school's financial stability improved when Joab Austin, a wealthy Austinburg merchant, pledged a twenty-five thousand dollar endowment for G.R.I. if trustees agreed to relocate school facilities to the north end where he conducted business. The trustees agreed with the proposal and after transporting the two-story structure a distance of three miles, they renamed the school the Grand River Institute.[5]

In 1840 G.R.I. followed Oberlin's example by opening its doors to females. It was hoped that the Women's Department would improve enrollment and financial problems. In addition to improving enrollment, the curriculum, and its financial status, the friends of G.R.I. broadened the school's educational objectives, aiming to provide both men and women with a college preparatory education in the same classroom. In 1842 the Reverend Thomas Tenney, a Dartmouth graduate, replaced Ralph Walker as principal of G.R.I. and it was Tenney, subsequently, who became Cowles's close associate in the fall of 1843.[6]

The approximately thirty girls under Cowles's supervision in the Women's Department received part of their instruction in the male Classical and English Departments. Cowles taught such courses as mathematics, physiology, and vocal music.[7] Cowles also incorporated informal discourses on moral character into her classroom presentations, which greatly pleased her students' parents and won her the sincere respect of a great many young scholars. She had a familial and compassionate rapport with students of all ages and classes, and a self-assured, forceful presence that many students never forgot.

Outside the classroom Cowles vigorously reasserted her Garrisonian principles and renewed her efforts in the abolition field. Prior to the mid-1840s, Cowles's successful organization of the Ashtabula County Female Anti-Slavery Society represented her most notable contribution to the cause. From approximately 1837 to 1845, in the wake of finishing her education at Oberlin, securing an instructorship at Portsmouth, and then tackling the responsibilities of the G.R.I. Women's Department, Cowles had little time to devote to abolitionism. Although she occasionally addressed local anti-slavery groups during her first years at G.R.I., her total involvement in abolitionism was negligible between 1837 and 1845.

Although Cowles voiced her Garrisonian viewpoints much more strongly after 1846 than in the previous decade, she had followed the Garrisonian banner, however passively, for over a decade. In 1834 she had endorsed immediate, moral abolitionism as secretary of the Austinburg Young Ladies Intellectual Society. While attending Oberlin she had sided openly with the Garrisonians against exclusion of women from active membership in the American and Foreign Anti-Slavery Society (AFASS). She also opposed the AFASS's policy of political rather than moral abolitionism. As a Garrisonian, she continued to follow the moral suasionist tactics of the original American Anti-Slavery Society, in addition to propagating the rights of women in the abolition sphere. In accord with the sentiments of the national society, Cowles promoted the viewpoint that the educational effects of strictly moral suasion would eventually lead to emancipation and that, in this educational process, women could and should take a leading role.

Voicing her beliefs in an address to a female anti-slavery society in 1843, Cowles emphasized that the first responsibility of an abolitionist was to become fully aware of all the facts concerning slavery. She explained her point in detail:

> We need to understand the subject—we want to acquaint ourselves with the subject of slavery in its length & breadth; height & depth. The character and consequences of slavery should be perfectly familiar to us; & the plans proposed for its discontinuance. We need to understand fully the connection of the A[merican] Church with Slavery—its moral influ-

ence upon the oppressed & oppressor; its physical sufferings—its mental & moral degredation *[sic]*. We need to know its political bearings[—]how far and in what way we in the nominally free states are involved; & the part we take in sustaining it; & the exact relation wh[ich] Congress sustains. We want to understand its character; as it has existed in other nations; & in days gone by. . . .

After abolitionists became fully versed in the facts concerning slavery, Cowles maintained that they should then become public moral educators. She explained that since "Ignorance is the cause of indifference, [and] ignorance is the parent of prejudice," the abolitionists's role was to educate the nation about the facts of slavery and thus to convert ignorant pro-slaveryites into educated, moral abolitionists.

Since Cowles was well aware that the general public frowned upon women who stepped out of their traditional roles concerning public matters, she maintained that this simple formula for emancipation was especially applicable to women. In the first place, Cowles regarded the slavery question as a moral matter and, since women were the traditional custodians of morality, they were properly within their sphere to take a direct, vocal role in trying to correct the immorality of human bondage. Despite such logic, Cowles warned that women who engaged in the educational process of moral suasion would encounter public scorn and contempt. They would hear that they were out of their proper places. Citing the Boston women abolitionists who endured disruptive riots and the contempt of their own sex, and placing Maria Weston Chapman at the head of the moral aristocracy, Cowles's point was well made:

> We are not strangers to that public sentiment wh[ich] says let womens influence be felt indirectly. . . . As rational beings, we have naught to do with such suasion. We seek not indirect action. The cause wh[ich] demands our efforts; demands the energy and sympathy of the soul exhibited in direct action.

Although she admitted the necessity of fund raising and sewing circles, she emphasized that the primary task of an anti-slavery society, male or female, was to agitate collectively in behalf of the slaves through moral suasion.

Cowles's prior references to the role of church and state in sustaining slavery revealed, in part, her Garrisonian attitude toward such institutions. Although she believed that religion should stand firmly on the principle "love they neighbor as thyself," she denounced the

church for having "clothed itself in the garb of selfishness, avarice &
wickedness."[8] Her views resembled those of Garrisonian Stephen S.
Foster, who bitterly denounced the American church and clergy in his
Brotherhood of Thieves, for turning their backs on the evils of slavery.[9] In Cowles's opinion, the American church was "as deeply im-
bued in the sin of slavery as was Pilate in the murder of Christ . . . &
in washing their hands, they make themselves about as pure as he
did."[10] Likewise, Cowles was convinced that if the Bible sanctioned
slavery, as some churches maintained, then the Bible ought to be
rejected. Significantly, however, instead of rejecting the Bible as a pro-
slavery document, Cowles believed that pro-slavery churches misin-
terpreted the Bible.

Cowles's view of the moral character of the nation as a whole was
no less denunciatory. Drawing upon the sentiment of Theodore
Weld's *American Slavery As It Is,*[11] Cowles revealed dramatically her
thoroughly Garrisonian conclusion that the whole moral fiber of the
nation needed reform:

> Now the storm is not only gathering but the heavens are black with
> frowning aspect & vengeance seems ready to burst upon our guilty
> nation; nor need we think to escape; for our apathy & indifference call
> aloud for retribution. Gladly w[oul]d we turn from the dark prospect, but
> whither shall we look? To the South? If one particle of humanity remains
> in the soul; it must sicken at the sight of this vast moral prison house. . . .
> We look to the North; the East; & the West for relief—do we find it? . . .
> They tell us; that the whole heart is sick; corruption has infested the whole
> nation. There is no soundness in it. With the prominent facts of the day
> before us; we cannot but admit that there is truth in the sentiment. . . .

Furthermore, she warned that if the spirit of righteousness did not
descend speedily upon the nation, there were grounds for the fear that
Civil War could give men the opportunity to "make a post-mortem of
our government, its constitution, & its laws."[12]

Although Cowles was not an active member of the Ohio Anti-
Slavery Society, nor of the Ashtabula County Female Anti-Slavery
Society between 1836 and 1845, during those years her Garrisonian
sentiments remained undiminished.[13] Moreover, in spite of her infre-
quent involvement in formal societal activities, Cowles kept abreast of
anti-slavery developments in both the East and West and monitored
the growth of political abolitionism.[14] She especially admired Maria
Weston Chapman, who as a leader in the Massachusetts Anti-Slavery

Society, endured the threats of mobs and riots for her unwavering support of Garrison. Chapman's anti-slavery fairs in Boston, her advocacy of peace, and her full support of women as anti-slavery lecturers, were an inspiration to Cowles as well as to many other anti-slavery women.[15] For Cowles, the name of Maria Weston Chapman would "stand when those of heroes & warriors . . . [would] be lost in the rubbish of time."[16]

Likewise, during her years of essentially passive abolitionism, Cowles began to regard Benjamin Lundy and William Lloyd Garrison as martyrs for the anti-slavery cause. Their individual, pioneering thoughts, she believed, would move the world onward by "expanding in various directions ultimately moving generations."[17] Noting that, " 'the world crucifies before it defies its saviors,' " Cowles compared Lundy and Garrison with Copernicus and Galileo because they were persecuted for spreading unpopular ideas accepted by succeeding generations. "The fools madmen—& fanatics of one age," Cowles believed, "are the wise—sane & conversative of another. Persecution & death ever have awaited the men who lived before their time." Such was the case with a Lundy and a Garrison whose "song of freedom," Cowles wrote, "shall be heard th'o the time is not yet."

Well situated at G.R.I. and in the Austinburg community by 1846, Cowles was again in a position to take a leading, active role in local anti-slavery work. Furthermore, questions concerning Texas, the Mexican War, and the Ohio Black Laws, prompted abolitionists to voice their opinions more strongly than in the previous decade. Such controversies prompted Cowles to assert her Garrisonian viewpoint while broadening her societal involvement after 1846. Whereas almost ten years earlier, her anti-slavery endeavors were local and focused principally on the county level, her renewed involvement included participation in some national abolition affairs. Given Cowles's renewed participation and the increasing needs of state and national abolition societies for active members, she might have subsequently supplemented her local anti-slavery prominence with substantial national recognition.

Cowles fell short of achieving wider recognition for two principal reasons. One was her dedication to teaching and the other was her affection for Ohio. While love of homeland kept her from large-scale involvements with the American Anti-Slavery Society in the East, the lure of academia and other reform interests prevented her from donating more time to local abolition work. Nevertheless, Cowles's role in local abolitionism in the 1840s was notable, although her significance for the cause nationally was limited to that of a western grassroots propagator of eastern Garrisonian ideas.

As an Ohio Garrisonian, Cowles conducted most of her organizational work through the Western Anti-Slavery Society (WASS). The WASS developed out of the 1840 dispute in the AASS ranks over the society's tactical approach to its long-range abolition goal. The upshot of the controversy was the formation of a rival group, the American and Foreign Anti-Slavery Society (AFASS). It endorsed Liberty Party abolitionism and did not allow female members to hold office. The original AASS, led by Garrison, emerged from the schism as strictly moral abolitionists and in favor of women holding office. As a result of the eastern schism, Ohio abolitionists also split ranks. By 1845, the WASS, originally entitled the Ohio American Anti-Slavery Society, was an almost exact replica of the eastern Garrisonian group. The WASS resolved at its founding in 1844 to condemn American churches for their neglect of anti-slavery work and requested its eastern counterpart, the AASS, to send to Ohio such lecturing agents as Abby Kelley. By its first anniversary in 1845, the increasingly radical western Garrisonian group disavowed any sympathy with political abolitionism and adopted the Garrisonian motto, "No Union with Slaveholders." In addition, the WASS condemned Liberty Party men for lifting politics above morality, vowed to give no allegiance to the United States government and constitution, and to change pro-slavery sentiment by the power of moral force.[18]

One of the prime movers of the WASS, and subsequently one of Cowles's personal friends, was Abby Kelley. As a Garrisonian agent she was present at the society's first anniversary meeting and helped to steer the group firmly into the Garrisonian camp.[19] With the help of her traveling companions, Jane Elizabeth Hitchcock, Parker Pillsbury, and Stephen S. Foster, Kelley also established the Salem (Ohio) Anti-Slavery Bugle as the WASS's weekly newspaper.[20] Born to a Massachusetts Irish-Quaker family in 1810, Abby Kelley grew to be an attractive, tall, blue-eyed, brown-haired woman. By reading Garrison's Liberator, Kelley was converted to abolitionism and from 1835 to 1837, she served as the Lynn (Massachusetts) Female Anti-Slavery Society's secretary. Then, at the first women's anti-slavery convention in New York in 1837, Kelley met Sarah and Angela Grimké. The three Quaker women became mutally encouraging friends owing to their shared convictions that women should speak publicly for the abolition cause. The following year, after Kelley delivered an impressive speech to a mixed audience at the second women's anti-slavery convention in Philadelphia, Theodore Weld strongly urged Kelley to become an abolitionist lecturer. Believing that to " 'improve mankind' was 'the only object worth living for,' " and regarding the vocation as a call from God, Kelley entered the lecturing field.[21]

In September 1838, Kelley joined Garrison in founding the New England Non-Resistance Society and as a lecturer in 1839 she spoke in New England, Pennsylvania, and western New York. With her booming voice and piercing eyes, she converted many to the cause in spite of the persecution she endured as a female. Kelley's nomination and subsequent appointment to the AASS Business Committee in 1840, was one contributing factor to the formation of the rival organization, the AFASS. Kelley was an unwavering Garrisonian—against the Liberty Party and against the new organization. When her converts began to join the Liberty Party instead of the AASS, she decided to travel west, where she subsequently met Cowles, in order to fight the Liberty Party and the AFASS more effectively. Kelley was also a comeouter and a disunionist, believing that people should come out of, or disassociate themselves with churches and other institutions that did not take a strong anti-slavery stand. As a disunionist she believed that the United States should be peacefully dissolved in order to disassociate the free North from the pro-slavery South. In short, she disclaimed allegiance to both church and state, regarding them as the principal supporters of human bondage.

Voicing these views in her lectures, Kelley was regarded by the general public as an arch-radical Garrisonian. Even anti-slaveryites were often offended by her forceful denunciations of both church and state.[22] Because Kelley often traveled with men such as Garrison, Parker Pillsbury, and Stephen Foster, rumors of her impropriety were many, if unsubstantiated.[23] Her marriage on 21 December 1845, to the radical anti-clericalist, Stephen Foster, did not in the least change her ways or improve her public image. As a. lecturing team Stephen and Abby Kelley Foster were a favorite among audiences because of their novelty and talent for public speaking, in spite of their radical comeouter and disunionist proclamations.

When Abby Kelley Foster arrived in Ohio in 1846 she looked forward to meeting Cowles as a kindred spirit. Even before their initial acquaintance in February, Foster regarded Cowles as "one of those who shrink involuntarily from political or ecclesiastical fellowship direct or indirect with those who make merchandise of God's image."[24] Foster hoped that Cowles would help her both to discredit the Liberty Party and to convince local societies to adopt disunionism. In fact, Cowles agreed with the Western Anti-Slavery Society's full-scale adoption of the Garrisonian disunion motto and looked forward to meeting Foster with equal regard.[25] As the Ashtabula County Female Anti-Slavery Society secretary in 1846, Cowles informed Foster where the coming quarterly meeting would be held, welcomed the well-known lecturer to the gathering, and expected "great times" at the affair.[26]

During the week before Cowles met Foster, Ashtabula County was reportedly "all alive on the anti-slavery question."[27] Cowles and other anti-slavery women, particularly Cowles's old friend Betsey Hudson, disagreed about the efficacy of adopting disunionism in the county-level societies. Cowles was firmly convinced, in spite of reading William Goodell's works assuming the viability of the Constitution, that the latter document clearly sanctioned human bondage and should therefore be rejected. Hudson, on the other hand, whose sentiments were like her husband's in the American and Foreign Anti-Slavery Society, urged Cowles to read Lysander Spooner's *Unconstitutionality of Slavery* with a less biased mind.[28] Local disagreement about the best road to abolition and the increasing popularity of the Liberty Party in the Reserve were stirring issues. Ashtabula County's anti-slavery women looked forward to a lively quarterly meeting in Morgan township on 5 February, with featured speakers Stephen and Abby Kelley Foster.

Although the meeting was on the whole uneventful, the Ashtabula County women were receptive hosts and Cowles regarded the affair as a great success. Afterwards she entertained the Fosters in Austinburg for five days during which time she convinced S. W. Streeter, Austinburg's Congregational minister, to allow the Fosters to speak in the church. Fearing that conservative church members would object to admitting controversial speakers, Cowles was delighted that Streeter did not consult the congregation before granting the Fosters permission to lecture.[29] The couple impressed the Austinburg congregation with their Sunday speeches, during which only a few of the church members went home. The Reverend Streeter was particularly impressed, thanking the guest lecturers for "the light given to him."[30] Perhaps Cowles was the most pleased of all Austinburgers, and after the Sunday speeches she intimated to Cornelia, "Abby & Foster are all that is noble & excellent; I love them very much; . . ."[31]

In the spring of 1846, the Fosters continued their lecturing tour in various northeastern Ohio communities, spreading their disunionist ideas and denouncing the Liberty Party. With Cowles's recommendation, they were even allowed to speak to the Oberlin anti-Garrisonians.[32] Wherever the Fosters traveled, they made distinct but differing impressions upon their western audiences. At Oberlin they were given a cordial enough welcome, but according to the Hudsons, the Fosters arrived at the inconvenient time of a revival, diverting the town's religious spirits to other matters. The Hudsons, who were exceedingly interested in Abby Kelley Foster, were skeptical of the lecturer's viewpoints and did not hesitate to inform Cowles of their disapproval.[33]

Betsey Hudson admitted, though perhaps not literally, that she liked Cowles a little less for "running headlong" into the errors of what Hudson termed "Abbyism."[34] Her particularly unfavorable opinion of Abby Foster stemmed from her belief that she had told deliberate untruths about Timothy Hudson during an Oberlin address filled with multiple vulgarities. Timothy Hudson, who was only slightly more sympathetic than his wife, reported to Cowles that he thought Foster was a hypocrite. Disagreeing with Cowles, he argued,

> You speak enthusiastically of Mrs. Foster. In part I go with you—in part I do not. That she is a person of powerful mind & of deep devotion to the cause of the bleeding slave I believe & feel most happy to say so. That she is doing great good I rejoice to say also—That she is an accurate reasoner— that her positions are all sound—that she is charitable, kind, fair & at all times truthful—I do not believe. She is doubtless a charming woman when she pleases to be so in the social circle. But I have the testimony of one who has long known her that she is at times vulgar enough.[35]

Although Foster had not favorably impressed the Hudsons, they believed that she had convinced Cowles to enter the lecturing field. In March 1846, Hudson heard that Cowles planned to become a public lecturer in the footsteps of Abby Kelley Foster. Although Hudson's information was only rumor, he revealed his deep admiration for Cowles with sincere words of encouragement:

> I am glad to hear that one so able as our old friend is opening her lips for

the dumb. On the propriety of the cause I have nothing to say. But if you feel it to be your duty to "cry aloud & spare not" God forbid that I should lay a straw in your way. . . . [Y]ou would make a glorious speaker,—. . . your fervent feelings, your . . . language, your writhing sarcasm—your sympathy with all that is noble . . . your magnificent person. . . . I would go a hundred miles to hear you. You'll beat Abby to nothing when you have a little experience. I'd rather meet a tropical tornado & Niagara falls to boot than to meet you as a public adversary.[36]

Although many in the Fosters's Ohio audiences would have agreed with the Hudsons's unfavorable viewpoints, the lecturing couple nevertheless seemed to convey their message successfully in certain localities. In Salem, Ohio, for example, where Liberty Party supporters and non-political abolitionists gathered to hear the Fosters, Levi Sutliff of Trumbull County interjected that the Liberty Party was anti-slavery's greatest accomplishment. Reportedly, Stephen Foster gave a rebuttal that convinced the majority present that the United States constitution was a pro-slavery document and that therefore, supporting the Liberty Party was indirectly supporting a pro-slavery government.[37]

In other Ohio communities, such as Elyria, Chagrin Falls, and Farmington, the Fosters began to count a handful of converts to comeouterism and disunionism. Perhaps no place was more receptive to the couple's message than Ashtabula County where the Cowles sisters acted as an effective liaison. Both Martha and Betsey repeatedly told their acquaintances to listen to the Fosters first and then to decide about the truthfulness of their message. In return, Foster was thankful, telling Cowles in March 1846, "God bless the women of Ashtabula Co[unty] for their efforts to enlighten their neighbors."[38] By April the reputation of the Ashtabula County anti-slavery women was recognized even in Cleveland. After the Fosters lectured in that city the *Cleveland American* reported,

> . . . everyone came in for their share of abuse. None escaped. If a man belonged to one of the pro-slavery churches, however correct his own individual sentiment, still he was none other than a pro-slavery man. No one could live in our nation, and be anti-slavery, unless he took his cue from Abby. . . . Indeed we know of no association of professed anti-slavery persons who escaped the lash of their tongues, except a little knot of professed anti-slavery women in the county of Ashtabula.[39]

Abby Kelley Foster was particularly thankful for Betsey Cowles's comradeship and returned it in kind by inviting her to come on the return trip to the East in order to attend the twelfth anniversary meeting of the AASS. Foster believed that the Ohioan was destined to "go forward in this great work of redeeming mankind."[40] Indeed, Foster would have rejoiced to see Cowles in the lecturing field. While Cowles reflected on such a possibility for the future she prepared to travel east with Foster to attend the anniversary in May 1846.

At the anniversary in New York, Cowles finally met other eastern Garrisonians for whom she had immense admiration. Although Maria Weston Chapman was prevented from attending the convention for health reasons, Cowles became acquainted with other well-known abolitionists such as Samuel Brooke. Brooke was an anti-slavery agent who supplied AASS publications to the WASS for distribution and sale. Cowles was also appointed to the AASS Business Committee with Parker Pillsbury, William Lloyd Garrison, Samuel Brooke, Oliver and Mary Ann Johnson, and the Fosters.[41] The following week Foster escorted Cowles to the New England Anti-Slavery Society annual convention in Boston. There, Cowles was again named to the Business Committee, consisting mainly of the same persons serving on the AASS Business Committee.[42] One of the main topics of discussion at both of the anniversaries in addition to disunionism and comeouterism, was United States involvement in the Mexican War. The conferees denounced it as a pro-slavery conflict. Although Cowles did not participate very vocally in the convention proceedings, except perhaps in the privacy of the Business Committee sessions, she nevertheless became acquainted with eastern organizational work and its anti-slavery personnel.

Inspired by the eastern conventions, Cowles launched an unprecedented anti-slavery campaign upon her return to Ohio. She organized anti-slavery fairs in the fall of 1846, in the spring and fall of 1847, and another in the spring of 1849. With Jane Elizabeth Hitchcock, co-editor of the *Anti-Slavery Bugle,* Cowles distributed and sold AASS literature supplied to her by Samuel Brooke.[43] In 1847, Cowles again served as secretary of the Ashtabula County Female Anti-Slavery Society and was appointed to the WASS Business Committee in 1848. In the following year she served as the WASS recording secretary.

In the summer of 1846, Cowles continued to collaborate with Abby Kelley Foster in spreading disunionism and attempting to discredit the Liberty Party for trying to appropriate the fruits of moral abolitionist labor. Their enthusiasm for disunion was particularly fired by the Mexican War. They believed the war was intended to lead to the expansion of slave territory, as discussed at the eastern anniversaries.[44] They also tried to guide the work of local societies by informing them of what effective anti-slavery work ought to be.[45] Both women agreed that fund-raising was important for the cause. But the real work, they believed, ought to be direct agitation against the Liberty Party's efforts to capture the support of supposed moral abolitionists. According to Cowles and Foster, such misguided abolitionists could help to change the nation's pro-slavery government more effectively by becoming disunionists and comeouters instead of political pawns. Cowles urged Ohio's county societies to adopt the disunionist motto for display on county flags, and Foster even requisitioned a disunionist song for Cornelia Cowles to sing at local meetings.[46]

Although Cowles and Foster agreed upon the major tenets of Garrisonian abolitionism, Foster's intent to discourage political abolitionism conflicted with Cowles's desire to help repeal the Ohio Black Laws. The Black Laws, which regulated the legal rights and social conduct of blacks, were, according to Cowles, a form of "oppression in our nominally free states."[47] To aid in their repeal, she used funds gathered at the annual Ashtabula County Female Anti-Slavery Society meeting and fair in 1846 to finance the publication of an anti-Black Law paper entitled *Plea for the Oppressed*. Written by Cowles and published by Jane Elizabeth Hitchcock, the paper consisted of three polemical sheets published monthly from December 1846 to February 1847. Cowles's use of society funds in order to repeal the Black Laws was questionable to some staunch Garrisonians. But Liberty Party supporters and moral abolitionists were more cooperative and tolerant of each other in the West than they were in the East.

Parker Pillsbury, who was present at the Ashtabula County Female Anti-Slavery Society's quarterly meeting in Austinburg, witnessed the proceedings of that gathering which led to the decision to publish an anti-Black Law paper. According to Pillsbury, the project was endorsed by the Whig candidate for governor, William Bebb, and encouraged by a group of Liberty Party men whose meeting was concurrent with the ladies society meeting. Since the anti-slavery women adopted the project, Pillsbury accused them of being controlled by those who ought to be their political adversaries.[48] Nevertheless, Cowles issued an appeal in the *Bugle* stating that funds from the annual meeting and fair in Jefferson would be appropriated to the publication of three numbers of the anti-Black Law paper.

Illustrative of Cowles's nonpartisan approach to benefit free Ohio blacks as well as slaves was her public statement in the *Bugle,* which read,

> All friends of the slave *"of every persuasion"* are respectfully invited to attend. Come one, come all, friend and foe—come-outer and come-inner.
>
> Those who think every movement of the professed friend of the slave, only rivets his chains, come, that you may be confirmed—Those who blush for woman, that she is thus out of her sphere, come and see how she looks, that you may blush the more; . . .
>
> Those who think nothing is done, come and see the nothing—. . .—those who think much is accomplished come and see—"great is the work." Those whose superior wisdom looks upon us with contempt, come and see our folly—the contrast will enable you to appreciate even more highly your own superiority.[49]

After requesting those who condemned to come and condemn intelligently, Cowles continued her appeal with characteristic sarcasm—a talent that won her the affection of anti-slaveryites of every persuasion.

> Those who call us Abby Kellyites do just come and see what a company of such "ites" will do; only think of it, if only one creates such a stir in community—what will a whole company do! Don't lose the sight, come and see.
>
> Those who call us Garrisonians take your shield in hand; carefully peep over or under it; see how such "oos" look; those who call us Liberty Party—buckle on the whole political armor; come and stand your ground manfully.[50]

Although the *Plea for the Oppressed* earned the initial skepticism of Parker Pillsbury, it seemed, according to Jane Elizabeth Hitchcock, to be highly appreciated and much needed. Hitchcock claimed that if the Black Laws were not repealed by 1 March 1847, the "Slavocrats" in Mercer County threatened to expel their black residents by violence.[51] The resulting *Plea,* however, was more of a moral polemic for disunion and comeouterism than a political tract benefiting the Whig or Liberty Parties as Pillsbury and other eastern Garrisonians had feared it would be. In the *Plea* Cowles referred neither to specific Black Laws nor to particular political parties. Instead, she mocked the characteristics of nominally free Ohio for having denied the rights of men to twenty-five thousand of its citizens. She condemned the Ohio legislature for listening to propositions that would enslave Ohio citizens, and for its "past obsequiousness in favor of and cringing servility" to the neighboring slave states, and for its willingness to do the "dirty work of slavery. . . ."[52]

Cowles connected the state of Ohio with the perpetuation of slavery and concluded:

> So long as Ohio constitutes a part of a slaveholding government, is it no wonder that she is what she is; and we think it not presumptuous to predict that if she remains subservient to a slaveholding power, her downward course in moral principle, and subjugation of principles of freedom and humanity will be in geometrical ratio. Proposing to sell her own citizens, and fighting for slavery, is all consistent with an abiding "union with slaveholders." Our country! To her how applicable the language of inspiration: "Babylon the great is fallen, is fallen," and another voice from heaven is saying, "Come out of her, my people, that ye be not partakers of her sins, and that ye receive not of her plagues."[53]

Despite Cowles's sincere anti-slavery intentions for the *Plea*, the news of Parker Pillsbury's initial observations of the affair that financed the paper created some doubt among eastern Garrisonians about Cowles's ability to use anti-slavery funds in a manner they approved. According to Foster, whose faith in Cowles remained essentially unshaken, Maria Weston Chapman feared that Cowles's fair "went to build up our worst foe and if so it had better never been."[54] Nevertheless, Foster encouraged her to hold annual fairs, but cautioned her to hold them "with a definite understanding of the specific object you intend to promote and then let those help who will—In this way the Boston fair receives much aid from its enemies, or rather, from the enemies of the cause which it promotes. . . ." Then, after Foster inquired about the *Plea* and requested to examine its contents, she further advised Cowles, "*You will say funds are of secondary importance*—But their disposal is a sign—We judge of the heart through the conduct of the hand and 'tis a pity, aye worse: almost a crime in us to [think?] that Slavocrats use our money—I do not think they do in your case."[55]

The petty bickering about the disposition of funds within the eastern Garrisonian circle may have discouraged Cowles from working more closely with the national society. In any case, in the fall of 1846 Cowles increased her activity in WASS affairs, and worked closely with Jane Elizabeth Hitchcock Jones of the *Anti-Slavery Bugle*. Jones, who grew up in New York's revivalistic "burned-over district," was one of Abby Foster's lecturing protegés. In 1845, Jones journeyed to Salem, Ohio, with a group of anti-slavery lecturers that included Benjamin Smith Jones whom she married on 13 January 1846. The couple stayed in Ohio to edit the *Anti-Slavery Bugle*. Jones, like Cowles, believed that women could be equal to men scholastically and treasured her ability to earn an independent living.[56] Throughout 1847, Cowles assisted Jones with the WASS anti-slavery book agency in Salem and helped organize several WASS fairs in 1847 and 1848.[57]

Cowles's association with Jones did not end with business matters. Their mutual interests in female education and women's social welfare drew them closer together in spirit and friendship than either of them were to their mutual friend Foster.[58] Significantly, after the *Plea* incident and Foster's temporary retirement from the lecturing field in early 1847 due to pregnancy, Cowles's personal and formal association with most of the eastern Garrisonians diminished. Cowles and Foster corresponded until 1849 about various anti-slavery affairs, but their geographical separation and Cowles's decision not to enter the lecturing field prevented a closer relationship between the eastern and western Garrisonians.[59]

In the West, however, news about Cowles's anti-slavery projects and accomplishments spread beyond the inner circles of Garrisonian abolitionists. Her *Plea for the Oppressed*, for instance, attracted the attention of the American and Foreign Anti-Slavery Society. When the AFASS began to prepare an anti-Black Law work in 1848, Timothy Hudson, a member of the society's Executive Committee, asked Cowles to furnish the organization with data compiled previously for the *Plea*.[60] Likewise, and more notably, Frederick Douglass learned of Cowles's reputation partly through Cornelia, who sang and taught music for a time in Buffalo, New York, during the latter half of the 1840s. Cowles visited her sister, who supported Douglass's *North Star* in the summer of 1848 and during the journey became acquainted with the well-known black abolitionist. When the Anti-Slavery Friends of Western New York desired an "efficient female agent" to head an anti-slavery office in Rochester, New York, Douglass suggested Cowles as a suitable person for the position.[61] Her anti-slavery reputation was even carried as far west as Iowa where she was offered a seminary teaching appointment to "sow the seeds" of abolition.[62] Elsewhere, in Portsmouth, Ohio, Cowles's reputation was less favorable. There, she tried to circulate the *Bugle* with the aid of her sister-in-law's Portsmouth uncle, Samuel Dole. He subsequently inquired of his niece if all the Cowles family had "turned Infidels" since he had heard reports to that effect.[63]

In league with the Garrisonians, and in agreement with the general sentiments of Ohioans,[64] Cowles also agitated against the Mexican War. For Cowles and others, the war stood for two principal evils— the extension of slavery and the murder of innocent human beings. Coupling the anti-war cause with her pervasive stand against slavery, she recorded privately the poetic lines:

> Work thou on for the poor & suffering slave
> Though the great men should scoff & vile men should rave
> And may God Almighty this nation divide
> And for slaves and Mexicans quickly provide
> What vast ropes of glory shall round thee be thrown
> When the organ shall pour its deep mellow tone
> When blest joyful spirits shall sing of the free
> And the song rise up like the waves of the sea.[65]

Similar to her prose, which cast such visionary men as Galileo, Copernicus, Lundy, and Garrison in a martyrlike role, the poem may have reflected Cowles's hope that her unpopular anti-slavery beliefs would someday be recognized as truth and her efforts praised by future generations. Cowles also sponsored and circulated in Lake and Ashtabula counties an anti-war petition pledging its signatories to be against the Mexican War because the conflict would result in an extension of slave territory.[66]

Cowles revealed her strongest anti-war sentiments by writing a satiric playlet, mocking both President James K. Polk and General Zachary Taylor as pawns of United States expansionism after the bloody assault on the Mexican town of Monterey on 21 September 1846. The play's two characters, Uncle Sam and Zachary, are cast in employer-employee roles. Uncle Sam, the employer, explains that in order to please his "boys" who are "clamorous for more territory," he must take measures to get a good piece of his neighbor Mexico's farm.[67] Uncle Sam then enlists Zachary to kill the people of Monterey who are opposed to Uncle Sam's plan. Zachary, though, is reluctant to follow his orders, rationalizing that the people of Moneterey are innocent and that to kill them would be murder. Uncle Sam replies that once Zachary is enlisted he must carry out the orders or die himself and that if he attempts to leave Uncle Sam's service without permission he will be shot or hanged. Zachary then agrees to work for Uncle Sam for two hundred dollars a month. While Zachary is away performing the assigned task, Uncle Sam comments that if Zachary "does up the work well" he will be able to move into the white house on the hill.

When Zachary returns from Monterey he reports the battle results to his employer:

> In one room I found a mother & four children all mangled to pieces. In another, the mother was killed & an infant was sleeping in a cradle near her. In another room was an old man almost wild over the mangled body of his daughter. She was all that he had. One of our men had become acquainted with a young woman whom he loved & he begged me to spare the house in which she was.[68]

After Zachary assures Uncle Sam that the house was destroyed in spite of the man's love because it was in his employer's interests to do so, Uncle Sam exclaims in the last lines of the play, "You are the man for me *Sir* you shall have the Big Chair & the White house as soon as Jimmy's time is up."[69]

Although the play was probably never performed, Cowles revealed through its dialogue her aptitude for writing political satire with a simple but witty style. Zachary and Jimmy, the obvious literary counterparts of Zachary Taylor and James Polk, were portrayed simply as do-or-die pawns of land-hungry, murderous, Uncle Sam. As evidenced by Zachary's battle report, Cowles's major theme in the play was not the extension of slavery, but rather, the inhumanity of war itself.

The omission of a slavery-extension theme in the play indicated that Cowles's reform concerns were not focused exclusively on anti-slavery. She conducted peace meetings throughout the Mexican War and like many other moral reformers, continued to attend peace gatherings even after the war's end.[70]

As varied as Cowles's anti-slavery and anti-war efforts were, they remained for her only an adjunct, although an important one, to her career as an educator. Even though Cowles had the opportunity and personal mobility to relocate in the East, her affection and growing appreciation for Ohio kept her from doing so. She demonstrated her love for both education and the West in articles that she wrote for the

Child's Friend and Family Magazine. She had met its editor, Eliza Lee Follen, while on her trip to attend the AASS anniversary in May 1846. Follen, a long-time AASS member, shared with Cowles a mutual affection for youngsters and invited her to write for one of her several juvenile publications. The articles, published from September 1846 to September 1847, were written in an informal, simple style, appropriately formulated to capture the interest of a young child as well as to teach a moral lesson or illustrate the beauties of life. Four of the articles were written in letter form to "Frank," an unidentified Boston youngster Cowles met during her trip to the East in 1846.[71]

Using such major themes as human destiny, Ohio history, frontier life, and good versus evil, and incorporating brief anti-slavery and anti-war comments as well, Cowles recorded in the articles a rather complete composite of her life's philosophy and interests. Cowles believed that every human being and living organism of the earth existed to perform certain tasks fulfilling their individual destiny. Timothy Hudson, recalling this axiom when he anticipated Cowles's entry into the lecturing field on the side of his ideological adversaries, quoted some of Cowles's most cherished lines by an unnamed author: "Like as a star / That maketh not haste / That taketh not rest / Be each one fulfilling / Our God-given test."[72] In a "Letter to Frank," Cowles illustrated her philosophy by endowing animals and plants with human desires to fulfill their tasks:

> I saw the fields decked with flowers so bright and beautiful! each spear of grass, each blossom, each shrub and tree, hill, valley, and plain, seemed to say, "I have something to do," and each seemed intent upon doing it,— upon fulfilling its destiny: So said the little bird, the busy ant, and creeping insect.[73]

When the objects confronted other objects, which invited them to forget their tasks, each one resisted the diversionary temptations in order to fulfill their destinies. Thus, moralized Cowles, she and each child, like the "bird, beast, flower and insect, winds and waves," must " 'work away while we're able, work away, work away.' "[74] Employing a similar theme in another "Letter to Frank," Cowles stated her idealistic humanitarian philosophy more clearly:

> . . . If we are only doing something which will benefit the world, something which will make people happier and better; this every little child can

do. Let us make somebody happier every day we live; then we shall not live in vain, or look back upon life with sorrow.[75]

Cowles devoted another "Letter to Frank," to the subject of slavery. In the article, Cowles taught her lesson by telling the story of a fugitive slave woman who carried her young child to northern Ohio with the slavehunter's hounds not far behind. Desperate for freedom, the mother abandoned the child on a bridge in order to escape the nearing captors, only to be caught and hauled back into southern slavery. The child, though, was protected by its guardian angel, but the mother's guardian angel was helpless against the wicked spirit of slavery.[76] Such educational stories were indicative of Cowles's affection for children, her vocational strength, and of her personal humanitarian spirit.

Cowles based two of her letters to "Frank" on episodes from Ohio's frontier history, recalling the hardships and deprivations suffered by the state's early settlers. In one story, thematicizing the faithfulness of man's best friend, a settler, enroute from Monroe, Ohio, to Meadville, Pennsylvania, with only his dog for companionship, cut his foot accidentally in the middle of a vast forest. The injured traveler was only saved by the faithfulness of his dog around whose neck the man tied a message explaining his predicament. The dog hastened to the nearest settlement; the message was read; and the man was eventually saved.[77] In another tale recalling the hardships of frontier Ohioans, a New Connecticut settler was discovered frozen to death after attempting to reach his isolated family in a snow storm. The heroes of the story, "Dr. H." and "Joseph C," were characters drawn from Cowles's real past—Dr. Orestes K. Hawley and Joseph Cowles, two of Austinburg's earliest settlers. Reminiscent of the Western Reserve's past, the story also recalled the first Sabbath in New Connecticut, the importance of the Bible, the book of psalms, and of united friends and neighbors.[78] These stories conveyed Cowles's sense of appreciation of Ohio's New England heritage and the part her family and friends played in building a civilization from wilderness.

Lastly, Cowles's articles in the *Child's Friend* revealed her sense of civilization's progress and how that progress stripped man of compassion and generosity. Moreover, they revealed Cowles's preference for Ohio's wide open spaces and the honest friendship of isolated folks. Noting the influx of eastern mores into Ohio, Cowles reflected, "Every body is neighbor, and if one is in want, his neighbor supplies him if possible. It is otherwise when the customs of what is called 'refined society' are introduced. Then people become more selfish, the beauty and simplicity of real kindness are exchanged for the form. Forms must be, but shadow is not reality."[79] She explained further, "The more 'refined' society becomes, the more form without reality, I mean in what is called 'refined society.' I love the homely kindness of the 'log-cabin,' it is beautiful, for it is the true soul. It will share its last crust with its fellow."[80] To illustrate her point, she recalled a night she was stranded in the woods. Entertaining company, an aristocratic family living in a large frame house, refused shelter to Cowles and her companions, but the neighbors living in a log cabin that already held eighteen souls, gladly welcomed the stranded travelers. "But," concluded Cowles, "as our country grows older this *free soul* is lost for the form; but let me tell you, dear Frank, ceremony, can never compensate for want of soul. Give me the frank, whole soul of some of our log-cabins, and I can dispense with all of the 'Bon-ton' of Broadway and not feel myself the loser at all."[81] Cowles's beliefs concerning human destiny, her concern for man's welfare, her love for children, and her historical sense were conveyed in the *Child's Friend* articles. Taken as a whole, they represented a literary sketch of her life's major activities, interests, goals, and vocation.

Cowles's G.R.I. years were characterized most notably by her climactic involvement in abolitionism. But the slave's cause was only one among many reform causes in which she took an interest. In addition, by the late 1840s, strictly moral abolitionism had almost run its course. The ballot box, rather than female petitions, began to be regarded as a more effective way to end slavery. Anti-slavery women leaned more and more toward finding ways to influence elections rather than change the moral character of the nation. Since men were the only ones with the vote, many women reformers lent their efforts to sprouting women's rights groups. Many also channeled their energies through organized benevolent societies to help the poor and unfortunate in urban areas.[82] During the 1850s, Cowles's activities followed this trend. She participated fully in the heyday or moral suasion, but saw other avenues of reform which captured her attention during the remainder of her public life.

4
Women and Spirits

COWLES resigned from Grand River Institute in the fall of 1848. Dr. Lorenzo M. Whiting's persistence in urging his friend to teach in Canton might well have been among her reasons for doing so. Only a year Cowles's senior, the Canton physician enjoyed the company of knowledgeable, talkative ladies and his house was usually inundated with sociable boarding females. He regarded them as the best company for an aging, philosophical healer. Whiting's household was the scene of constant commotion due to the nature of a doctor's house-calling business and the untimely manner in which people fell ill. In his free time Whiting enjoyed playing chess, teasing his young boarders about marriage, extracting their opinions on social concerns, and experimenting with the curative effects of mesmerism.[1] Such an atmosphere delighted Cowles for she had welcomed the opportunity to visit the Whitings during her years at Grand River Institute.

Whiting and his wife, Mary, kept themselves well-versed on current events and trends. They were both decided abolitionists and leaned toward third party politics. The down-to-earth doctor, especially, regarded the strictly moral abolitionists of Cowles's type as too saintly. In addition to the subjects of abolition and politics, Whiting took an interest in the communitarian principles of Charles Fourier, following local plans for an associated community on the Ohio River and acquiring friends at the widely known Brook Farm experiment.[2] Although Whiting usually attended church services, mainly to please his wife, his stronger Sunday calling was to draft letters.

The Whitings's long and continued relationship with the Cowles family began in the early 1840s. Perhaps it originated when Cornelia Cowles retailed music in the Canton vicinity, or perhaps when Dr. Harry Wadsworth discovered the Canton doctor's similar interest in mesmerism.[3]. Whatever the origin, Cornelia and Betsey Cowles became favorite guests at the Whiting household. Between their visits, Whiting begged for their return and usually either one or the other sister arranged to call at the doctor's bustling home. Rarely though, despite careful planning, did the Cowles sisters manage to schedule coincidental visits. When Cornelia arrived she filled the house with music and laughter and practiced her "divinities and wiles"[4] upon the unsuspecting Stark County bachelors. When Betsey visited the Whitings, she tested the doctor's skills at chess, ice-skated, ate oysters to her heart's content, and engaged the doctor in long conversations about popular literature, temperence, abolition, politics, religion, and diverse domestic trivia. Through the years, Whiting became one of Cowles's most beneficent, as well as delightful acquaintances.

Cowles's quick wit and intellect no doubt impressed Doctor Whiting, but his wife and other local women were impressed with her talent for instructing their youth during her short visits. In the early months of 1848, several Canton women planned to procure Cowles's steady services teaching the children of approximately twenty families for a salary equal to that which she received from Grand River Institute.[5] Although that plan never came to fruition, in 1848 the Whitings's plan to have Cowles teach in the Canton vicinity finally succeeded. The near-by city of Massillon instituted a reorganization of its school system, and, through acquaintances Whiting was able to secure Cowles a position.[6]

The opportunity to teach in the newly reorganized Massillon schools must have been an attractive one for Cowles. Massillon, the largest community in Stark County, claimed three to four thousand inhabitants with an increasing school-age population.[7] Like many growing communities in the United States in the mid-nineteenth century, its numerous youth necessitated a change from the district school system, to a graded system. In the graded system students could attend sequentially a primary school, a grammar school, then a high school with the added benefit of receiving instruction from teachers who specialized in dealing with a particular age group or subject. This new trend in the administration of free Ohio public schools began in Akron in 1847. There it proved to be so efficient that in the following year provisions of the Akron school law were made available to any incorporated Ohio community. Subsequently, the Akron graded school system was imitated by other populous Ohio cities such as Massillon and in many other states as well.[8]

Organized on 23 October 1848, the Massillon Union School housed primary, grammar, and high school departments with a total average attendance of four hundred and fifty pupils. In the fall of 1848, Cowles accepted the position of teacher and principal in the grammar department with a generous annual salary of three hundred dollars, the highest salary paid to any of the Massillon female instructors. Interestingly, her male assistant, Charles Shreve, received only two hundred dollars annually[9]—a rare reversal of roles and salaries for the mid-nineteenth century.[10]

Cowles's employment in Massillon might have been longer and certainly much more pleasant had it not been for her strong response to the Ohio Black Laws. The 1848 Ohio legislature passed an Act which allowed black children to attend publicly supported common schools provided, "no written objection be filed with the directors signed by any person having a child in such school, or by an legal voter of such district."[11] In other words, if only one such person objected to Negro children attending the local common school, the students could be legally forced out of the classroom. These and other Ohio Black Laws had long been a source of utter contempt for Cowles. The situation so infuriated her that she wrote several anti-Black Law articles.

In December 1848, Cowles's first article appeared in the *Anti-Slavery Bugle*. In it, she emphasized that ultimate responsibility for the Black Laws lay not with the Ohio legislators, but rather their constituents, who voted politicians into office. She contended that since a "corrupt public sentiment," created the "impolitic, unconstitutional and wicked laws," they would stay on the books until public sentiment demanded their eradication.[12] She stated further that she was aware of dabbling in politics, but justified her right to encroach on this masculine sphere until all laws were just, equitable, and available to all.

Cowles's December article was not unlike her previous public pronouncements in the anti-slavery press. Had she been satisfied with its effect, her subsequent difference of opinion with some Massillonians might never have developed into a confrontation. When the common school law for blacks was put to the test in the Massillon Union School the veteran teacher was outraged. After years of arguing for the repeal of the Black Laws, Cowles decided it was time to change her course of action.

In a second letter to the *Anti-Slavery Bugle*, published in February 1849, Cowles described in detail the events that had taken place at the Union School regarding the disposition of Negro students. She urged that a suit be brought against the trustees to test the Black Laws in court. In the February letter Cowles explained that when the Union

School opened the previous October, eleven black students attended. All proceeded well for two or three weeks since, according to Cowles, the children and teachers had not imbibed the nation's " 'natural prejudice' " against color.[13] She continued contemptuously:

> Not so however with a *few* of the parents, who judging from their *frothing* had taken the color-phobia the 'natural' way; hence their convulsions were of the most pitiable kind; and their wailing most *bitter*. A *petition* demanding the expulsion of the colored children, by authority of the law which was passed last winter, 'providing for *better education*,' (what an insult) of the colored population of the State was circulated and some seventy or eighty signatures obtained.[14]

The petition, whose signatories included some prominent merchants involved with the Ohio Canal trade, was thus presented to the school trustees, who, according to Cowles, ignored it. Their noncompliance then "aroused the indignation of the 'very respectable petitioners' to the highest pitch."[15] Next, she related bitterly:

> A Lawyer, armed with the *majesty* of a most *majestic* law, was employed to vindicate the *majesty* of law. I have before heard of, but have never seen the *majesty* of law, and rods of terror wielded by lawyers. The lawyers threatened 'a writ of injunction on the house,' which had the desired effect. Every mouth was filled with 'writs of injunction on the house,' and 'on the funds;' until mighty fear seemed to pervade the community, as if there was danger of a 'writ of injunction' on the clouds and another on the sun, and another on the atmosphere, and perchance to vindicate the majesty of the law there may be a writ of some kind, or a States' warrant issued against the Almighty himself for presuming to create such a race; and that in the very face and eyes of the *very dignified* Legislature of Ohio.[16]

Certainly, the lawyers and laws did not frighten strong-willed Cowles, nevertheless the threat of enforcing the Black Laws sufficed to prevent Negro attendance. The black child in Cowles's class was told twice by authorities to stay home, but Cowles was led by "want of reverence for State or mob-law to bring her back to school. . . ."[17]

Furthermore, the banishment of the Negro students occurred on the day Bibles were presented to each academic department. "Of course," she sarcastically commented near the end of her February letter, "the lesson of 'Love thy neighbor' would fit admirably after such a practical lesson of moral beauty."[18] Hoping that her article would incite public outrage, Cowles urged her readers to bring a suit against the Massillon trustees in order to test the constitutionality of the black school law. Such action, however, was not necessary since the

1849 legislature repealed the Black Laws. Their repeal was the culmination of her crusade against racial prejudice, first in the Portsmouth Sabbath school, then with the *Plea for the Oppressed,* and finally with her articles from Massillon in the *Anti-Slavery Bugle.*[19]

Although Cowles finished the 1849 school term in Massillon, the Black Law incident probably strained her relationship with many school patrons and townspeople. At any rate, she arranged to teach in Canton after a long-anticipated vacation in the East. During her five-month trip Cowles helped with an anti-slavery fair in Boston. She also journeyed to Buffalo to rendezvous with Cornelia, next to the Catskills to stay for some weeks with her cousins, then to her birthplace in Farmington and to Bristol, Connecticut, to visit the New England Cowleses, and finally to other eastern cities.[20] As a whole the vacation proved to be a watershed in both Cowles's private concerns and professional career. After the trip she retained only nominal memberships in local and state anti-slavery societies. She continued to subscribe to the *Liberator*[21] but her leadership in Ashtabula County Female Anti-Slavery Society affairs diminished, as did her active role in the Western Anti-Slavery Society. Only occasionally after 1850 did Cowles venture to anti-slavery meetings and fairs, although she remained a dedicated supporter of the cause.

After her travels in the East, from November 1849 to March 1850, Cowles essentially rearranged her priorities. She spent more time in professional pursuits. Outside the classroom, she dabbled briefly in the women's rights movement, helped to relieve destitution in New York's Five Points district, and investigated spiritual phenomena. Her outside interests were rather diversified and they never received the same time and effort that she had devoted to the abolition movement in the 1840s.

Although the decline in Cowles's anti-slavery work might be attributed in part to her Massillon experience, it as most probably due to a number of other factors. Primarily, her professional duties and interests expanded around 1850 to include helping organize the Stark County Common School Association[22] and to presenting academic lectures at weekend teachers' institutes.[23] In addition, her appointment as superintendent of girls' grammar and high schools in Canton demanded a greater part of Cowles's energies than did her previous job in Massillon. Although she frequently referred to herself as just a "schoolmarm,"[24] she was one of the more prominent educators in the state.

Another factor in rearranging Cowles's extracurricular priorities was probably the open-minded company of the Whiting clan. Members of the Whiting household, usually teeming with spicy commentaries on current events, may well have discussed the famous 1848 Seneca Falls women's rights meeting since both Lorenzo and Mary Whiting supported enthusiastically the women's rights cause. Furthermore, they may have discussed the sensational Hydesville rappings since, as a typical supplement to an interest in mesmerism, Dr. Whiting displayed a similar fascination with the so-called spiritual manifestations.[25] The Whitings's enthusiasm and support for both women's rights and spiritualist investigations probably provided Cowles with encouraging company in discussing and participating in such matters.

In addition to Cowles's increased professional concerns and her keeping more frequent company with the Whitings, several other factors may have contributed to Cowles's diminished anti-slavery activities after 1850. First, in June 1849, her cherished friend Jane Elizabeth Jones relinquished the editorship of the *Anti-Slavery Bugle*. In May 1850, Jones launched a new career as a health and hygiene lecturer for women and subsequently enjoyed wide success throughout the state.[26] Immensely impressed with Jones's initiative, knowledge, and talent, Cowles persistently urged her students, family, and friends to attend Jones's lectures.[27] Second, her extended trip to the East was quite probably a factor, although the particular details of the journey she did not record. There she may have been more directly exposed to the problems of working women in urban areas, the destitution of the Five Points district, eastern literary circles, and even transcendentalism and spiritualist phenomena.

Although Cowles's brief participation in the early Ohio women's rights movement seemed an abrupt departure from abolitionist activities, she had long been cognizant of the inequalities women faced, particularly in the fields of education and labor. It was, however, not unusual for reformers, and certainly not for Garrisonians, to become active in women's rights.[28] Vocal female abolitionists were required many times to defend their rights to speak out for the anti-slavery cause. Cowles frequently mentioned these problems in her anti-slavery addresses and publications. She was also particularly aware of Abby Kelley Foster's difficulties in this regard since it was partly Foster's advocacy of women's rights that split the AASS. Her early belief that women, if properly educated, possessed the same capabilities as men in most activities may have given her a clear conscience about entering the abolition field as vocally and actively as many anti-slavery men. Particularly, Cowles emphasized that females should enjoy an education equal to that of men since only an inferior education made the female inferior in dealing with public affairs. The difference in abilities between men and women, according to Cowles, was rendered by different education. She believed that such was the case with blacks also.

In 1841 she voiced these exact sentiments in a letter to the Cleveland *Leader* describing the Oberlin graduation orations of a female and a Negro:

> [T]he first, (female) most clearly showing that women can think & express her thoughts—as well as attend to the important object of 'making a pudding'—that too she can be fitted for a higher sphere than a frizzled & frizzling toy for the parlor; & the latter (Negro)—can be so educated as to compare well with any ordinary class of college students. . . . It is becoming an admitted fact, that the above named classes can be profited by a course of study; as well [as] 'white males'.[29]

First as a student, then as a teacher, Cowles advocated improved female education—a goal which came to be one of the pleas of women's rightists. Furthermore, as part of the female labor force, Cowles experienced firsthand the inequalities of remuneration most working women received. The alleviation of this situation also came to be one of the strong resolutions of the early women's rightists. Thus, she carried her personal experiences and views into the early women's rights movement for she could not help but sympathize with a great many of its tenets.

As a women's rightist, Cowles admired such women as George Sand, whose *Consuelo and Countess Rondolstadt* she decided was "the most magnificent thing" she had ever read.[30] She also praised Margaret Fuller Ossoli, the well-known eastern trancendentalist and feminist. After Fuller's tragic death in June 1850, Cowles wrote an eulogy which reflected her own liberal-mindedness and appreciation for female achievements:

> With her [Fuller's] extended vision on all subjects—her richly cultivated intellect—her stars of knowledge & her perfect command of the reasoning faculties it was not strange that she should deviate from the orthodox theological tenets of the Puritan Fathers—wh[ich] was true in her case, & for which she suffered the penalty usually inflicted by the narrow-minded

& bigoted—that is [she] was denounced as heretical & skeptical. But not
so did she appear to those who distinguish between theology & Christianity. Testing her character by 'the fruits': she was preeminently a Christian.[31]

Although Cowles probably wrote this segment of the eulogy in part to
justify her own deviation from the faith of her Puritan Fathers, she
also recognized that Fuller was " 'one of the earliest as well as ablest
among A[merican] women to demand for her sex equality before the
law'," and that " 'her writings on this subject have the force wh[ich]
springs from profound reflection.' . . ."[32]

Generally, the early Ohio women's rights movement sprouted in the
1840s as a natural outgrowth of other reform movements. Women
such as Cowles played a major role in getting them started. Female
Garrisonians, in particular, displayed an interest in women's rights
since the role of their sex in organizational work became an issue.
Abolitionism especially, not only provided an organizational training
ground for women but also inspired some participants to demand for
their sex the equalities they sought in behalf of the Negro. Feminist
literature such as Mary Wollenstonecraft's *A Vindication of the
Rights of Women,* and the writings of Margaret Fuller Ossoli also
spread interest and aroused support for women's rights. The famous
meeting of women in Seneca Falls, New York, in 1848, gave courage
to a small group of Ohio feminists to follow suit the following year. In
the summer of 1849, these women gathered in Salem, Ohio, to plan
the first meeting devoted to female rights in the state.[33] Plans for the
gathering were announced, and a call was issued in the *Anti-Slavery
Bugle* in March and April 1850.[34]

Betsey Cowles was not among the eighty women who eventually
endorsed the meeting by attaching their signatures to the call, but her
friends Mary Whiting and Jane Elizabeth Jones were.[35] Cowles
learned about the meeting when she returned from the East, and
welcomed the opportunity to attend such an unprecedented reform
gathering in Ohio. Probably neither the Whitings nor Cowles
dreamed that the Austinburg teacher would be chosen as presiding
officer of the historic affair.

On 19 April 1850, an estimated two hundred participants and
observers gathered in the Salem Second Baptist Church for the meeting's first session.[36] While *pro tem* president Mary Ann Johnson read
the convention call, a five-woman nominating committee whose

members were suggested by Jane Elizabeth Jones selected permanent officers. The nominating committee consisted of Jane Elizabeth Jones and Jane Trescott of Salem, Emily Robinson of Marlboro, Josephine Griffing of Litchfield, and Martha Tilden of Akron.[37] Of these women only Jones knew Cowles personally and Jones was the likely candidate to have singled out Cowles for the position of president. However, the other committee members probably had some knowledge of Cowles's organizing talent, her public displays of courage and wit, and her success as a teacher and administrator. The choice of Cowles as president of such a female gathering may also have been intended to discount rumors that women's rightists were radical, fanatical characters. The convention women would have to depend on Cowles's leadership to disprove predictions that women could not implement parliamentary procedure properly without the aid of men.[38] The fact that she had considerable experience in appearing before groups of people may also have been a factor in choosing her as president. Cowles was not a radical or fanatical character, but rather a respected professional with courage and experience enough for the position. Cowles took charge of the historic convention proceedings and proved to be an able presiding officer.

The oppression women suffered under existing laws was the topic most frequently mentioned at the convention. Married women, the conferees learned, lost all legal identity. They were trapped as miserable dependents of their husbands, without rights to property or children. Women were required to obey laws, of which they had no part in the making; they paid taxes to a government that refused them representation; and they worked for grossly inferior wages. Many of the conferees agreed that because of such gross injustices, it was time for women to demand the elective franchise. Accordingly, a committee was appointed to draft a memorial to be presented to the Ohio legislature requesting that women be granted their right to vote and urging the legislators to eradicate oppressive and unjust laws concerning females.[39]

Jane Elizabeth Jones presented the keynote address entitled "The Wrongs of Woman." The former co-editor of the *Bugle* and accomplished abolition orator impressed the mixed audience with her self-assurance and eloquent presentation. Jones expounded upon women's legal and political restrictions. She also discussed woman's circumscribed sphere, which wrongly limited her educational opportunities, her vocational choice, and her financial reward. Women, she contended, were partly to blame for this degraded position because most women either did not recognize or did not care to change the social, legal, and political prejudices against their sex. Thus, organizing the minority of feminists who did care to claim their rights would be an awesome task. They would be ridiculed and outcast for presuming to step out of their accepted sphere.[40]

Although Jones's address echoed previous appeals for women's rights, in her message she struck one note that was of particular concern to Cowles—women's inferior wages. Jones pointed out that school teachers, girls in manual labor schools, and those employed in businesses received much less compensation for their work than did men. In some cases, females earned less than half the money men earned for performing equal tasks. More forcefully, however, Jones called attention to the mass of urban women who " 'work, work, work, stitch, stitch, stitch,' from early dawn till the midnight hour"[41] but received barely enough to keep themselves from starvation in a Christian country. The alleviation of degradation and misery among urban women later became one of Cowles's diverse reform interests in the 1850s, reflected by her work in New York's Five Points district.

As a whole, the two-day convention was fairly productive. In addition to producing a memorial to be presented to the Ohio legislature calling for women's suffrage, the conventioneers adopted twenty-two resolutions covering fairly well the gamut of feminist demands discussed at the meeting. They wanted equal educational and vocational opportunities, the elective franchise, and the erasure of women's legal, political, and financial disabilities. Furthermore, the convention participants resolved to hold annual meetings to promote their cause and monitor its progress. A Standing Committee, which did not include Cowles, was appointed to manage these arrangements for the coming year. Lastly, conventioneers prepared an "Address to the Women of Ohio," intended to arouse sympathy for the feminist cause.[42]

These documents and the meeting itself created little sympathy for the women's rights movement among those who were not already predisposed to reform sentiments. And although the memorial to the legislature ultimately carried over eight thousand signatures, the lawmakers proved unresponsive to the demand, failing to strike the word "male" from voting requirements by a vote of seventy-three to seven.[43] The participating women could only hope that the next year's meeting would strike a more responsive chord.

During the following year, Cowles busied herself mainly with the affairs of the Canton Union School. She also took time to investigate the extreme hardships of working urban women about which Jones had spoken at the Salem convention. She studied government reports and newspaper articles citing wage and hour statistics on urban workers. In Cowles's mind, and many agreed, the urban working situation forced women into the streets in order to ward off starvation—the circumstances bred destitution and destitution bred crime. Cowles presented the results of her study to the second women's convention held in Akron on 28 and 29 May 1851.[44]

The 1851 Akron women's rights convention generally resembled the preceding year's meeting in Salem. Many of the same women attended both affairs; however, men were allowed to participate in Akron. After the usual opening formalities, an ad hoc nominating committee reported the noted feminist and reformer Francis Dana Gage of McConnelsville as presiding officer. Cowles's companion, Mary Whiting, received one of the eight vice-presidencies and the Austinburger was reported as a member of the Business Committee responsible mainly for drafting resolutions. She was also scheduled to deliver her "Report on Labor," one of three special topic speeches featured at the meeting.[45]

Cowles delivered her address during the afternoon session of the second day of the convention. She began her report, which one sympathetic observer commented, "must have warmed the coldest heart,"[46] by contending that no nation had ever denied women the right to labor. She cited numerous examples featuring various nations that bestowed upon their women the right to drag a plow, tend cattle, tan hides, pound rice, pave streets, plant corn, or ply a needle for eighteen to twenty hours a day. She continued by focusing on the plight of Great Britain's 33,000 operative seamstresses, illustrating their miserable situations with cases in point. She explained how one elderly maiden and one widow employed as bonnet makers were required to work eighteen to twenty hours, seven days a week, to pay living expenses.[47] She cited another case of destitution involving a girl who supported her mother by sewing trousers from six in the morning until ten at night. The girl found that she could not survive on the money left after paying rent and thus was forced to sell herself. Of the thousands engaged in such work, according to Cowles, a virtuous one was rare because "they are driven into the streets for a miserable subsistence."[48] Cowles emphasized that poorly paid and overworked women swelled the tide of moral pollution and were also the makers of the "exquisite embroidery which so beautifully ornaments, and commands such prices in the princely establishments in Broadway."[49]

Cowles then turned her focus to the seamstresses of New York. By sewing fifteen to eighteen hours per day, she reported, some women earned from three to six dollars per month, although rent alone ranged from three to four and a half dollars per month. Rooms were generally in the "upper story of some poor, ill-constructed, unventilated house, in a filthy street, breathing a most sickly and deadly atmosphere, which deposits seeds of debility and disease with every inspiration."[50] She cited similarly sad statistics for women employed as straw braiders, artificial flower makers, cap makers, dressmakers, and domestic servants. She estimated the number of laboring women in New York alone amounted to 50,000, the majority of whom "only half breathe, (to say nothing of the living) . ." and if work could not be had they must "starve, beg, die, or worse."[51] The picture Cowles painted of urban female labor was indeed bleak. Given their situation, who could wonder, Cowles asked her audience, how immorality is bred in the city?

Cowles also devoted a small portion of her report to wages in the teaching profession. She noted that in the past seventy-five years it had become woman's peculiar province to teach. Public sentiment deemed it proper to her nature, and thus, teaching was one of the few professions open to women. Since women were deemed equally qualified to teach as men, but their labor could be had for half a man's wages, school administrators prefered to hire females as a majority of the teaching staff. With few other vocational opportunities, women assented to inferior wages. Cowles stated such was the reason that two-thirds of the Ashtabula County teachers were female in 1850. According to Cowles, females received an average wage of $6.85 per month while the average wage for males was over twice that amount— $16.50 per month. The statistics she cited for Cincinnati, Boston, and Connecticut showed similar differences in male-female wages in academic professions.[52]

The cause for the appalling statistics, Cowles concluded, was over-surplus in the market "with thousands to be employed, and only one, two, three or four occupations in which it is 'womanly' to be engaged. . . ."[53] She did not offer any concrete solutions to the female labor/wage problem in her report, although she did reprimand those women who jeered at the efforts of the convention to ameliorate the condition of women. The scoffers were ignorant, in Cowles's view, because they would not look at the reality of the situation. Women should instead help to create a public sentiment that would "administer justice and right." Her efforts would then help to redeem a "sin-racked world" and "restore that good which is lost by the long continued fall of our race."[54]

According to Cowles's comments in the Akron report, the role of women in the women's rights movement was similar to that of women in the abolition movement—to create a sympathetic public sentiment. On how best to accomplish this, she remained vague. She was too much of a visionary in the field of reform to worry about step-by-step action. Cowles's method of feminist reform was simply to be a sympathetic supporter, doing what good she could for the cause in her everyday way of life. Since in her mind she saw the reality of women's circumstances, she had no qualms about lending her support to the movement.

Before the Akron conventioneers adjourned, they made yet another attempt to give their cause some organizational continuity. They appointed a Standing Committee of six women and one man to plan another meeting the following year.[55] As a member of the Standing Committee, Cowles probably helped to schedule the next women's rights gathering in nearby Massillon and aided Mary Whiting in enlisting the active support of Dr. Whiting. At the 1852 convention in Massillon, the Canton physician helped to draft a constitution for a permanent women's rights organization, entitled the Ohio Women's Rights Association. The constitution made provisions for the establishment of local branches, annual meetings, and a membership open to any person interested in equal rights for all human beings in all endeavors. Cowles was given the honor of serving on the first Executive Committee of the new, and long-awaited association.[56]

The Executive Committee position marked Cowles's last active involvement in the Ohio feminist organization; thus, she did not attend the first anniversary of the Ohio Women's Rights Association held in Ravenna in the spring of 1853. Her credentials as a women's rightist were impressive.She was president of the first women's rights convention, a speaker and member of the Business and Standing Committees at the second, and chosen to serve on the Executive Committee for the Ohio Women's Rights Association at the third. In lending her active support for the cause from 1850 to 1852, Cowles helped to launch the pre-Civil War women's rights movement in Ohio.

Perhaps Cowles's most notable contribution to the women's rights cause was not her brief organizational involvement, but rather, her way of life. She was independent, successful, and respected by her peers. She was not the radical feminist character envisioned by most critics. Indeed, Cowles pursued the activity deemed most womanly and proper next to motherhood—she was a school teacher. Her profession and her growing popularity in the field lent her an air of conservatism and respectability. Thus, the women's rights cause no doubt profited from her brief association with it.[57]

Cowles might have continued her participation in the Ohio women's rights movement had she not decided to take another trip to the East in January 1853. Concerned about the destitute circumstances of many urban workers, Cowles journeyed to New York city to learn more about the living conditions especially in the Five Points slum. During her extended leave of absence from the Canton Union School, from January 1853 to April 1854, Cowles scouted New York visiting "Homes of the Friendless."[58] She also sewed for charities and attended the lectures of Charles Beecher, Lucy Stone, and Antoinette Brown.[59] Initially accompanied by Jane Elizabeth Jones and other Ohio friends, Cowles spent much of her trip with the well-known abolitionists Mary Ann and Oliver Johnson.

For Cowles the venture was not only educational but somewhat of a vacation. She had always loved to travel, visiting friends or relatives along her way. Accompanied or alone, the Ohioan learned the ins and outs of New York city life, both the beautiful and the stark. She patronized dress shops and millineries and bought presents for her western friends and family. Whiting generally received a letter from her every week and from them he ascertained that the "schoolmarm" seemed to be "going it in the great Babylon of America."[60] In January 1854, after her private Five Points mission was deemed a success, and her monetary resources exhausted, Cowles journeyed northward to spend the winter's remainder with her Catskill cousins. Extremely hospitable, Cowles's New York relatives furnished their Ohio cousin with all the comforts of home *sans* domestic chores and worries. "After being the servant of servants a whole life," Cowles wrote from Catskill, "it is very pleasant to enjoy the comforts of an easy home . . . [and] be waited upon."[61]

During her New York trip, Cowles also visited several reputable mediums, or persons supposedly able to communicate with the dead. Her interest in mediums arose in the early 1850s, when spiritualism, popularized by the notorious Hydesville rappings of 1848, gained numerous adherents. Indeed, many reformers, such as abolitionists and women's rightists, were among those interested in spiritualism. Many regarded it as more progressive and scientific than traditional religion. Cowles, as well as sister Cornelia, had been interested in the popular science of phrenology[62] and had followed the progress of Whiting's mesmeric healing since the early 1840s. Many people who endorsed mesmerism, which was based on the belief that all people contain a certain amount of electric fluid, were amenable to substituting the idea of spirit in place of electricity. Mediums claimed that spirits instead of electric fluid created unusual happenings termed spiritual manifestations.[63] A sympathetic acquaintance with such ideas predisposed Cowles as well as several of her family members and friends to believe in spiritualism, or organized attempts to communicate with the dead.

Purported spirits manifested themselves through mediums in various ways. Rapping or knocking in response to questions was the most frequent way of communication, but tipping furniture, throwing objects, or speaking in foreign languages through a medium were also typical forms of expression. Some mediums claimed to be spirit-writers, alleging that a spirit guided the medium's hand in response to participants' questions. By 1852, there were reportedly over 2,000 such spirit-writing mediums in the United States.[64]

Although Cowles never professed to be a medium, she did believe in their clairvoyant powers. She investigated their techniques, tested their abilities, and was convinced that they were indeed authentic and that their communications came from the spiritual realm. In her investigations, Cowles journeyed to Ravenna, Massillon, Cleveland, Rochester, New York, and other places purporting to have powerful mediums.[65] Cowles's acceptance of the mediums' power was partly a result of her strong desire to secure messages from her deceased father. Since these were what some mediums claimed to secure, she was not disposed to call them fake.

Many of the spirit communications Cowles received came through her niece, Helen Cowles Markham. Born in 1821 to Cowles's oldest brother, Markham experienced a turbulent childhood. She claimed that her parents mistreated her and vowed to move out of the family's Cleveland home as soon as she secured employment. This she did, supporting herself as a teacher until her first marriage to Dr. Franklin Markham in 1845. Markham developed powers as a medium shortly after her first husband's tragic death in a California shipwreck in

1850. Between her two marriages, Markham lived with her son in the Cowles's Austinburg homestead. Although well-treated by the Austin-burgers, Markham was generally stubborn, tempermental, and defensive regarding her clairvoyant abilities. In 1853, Markham married her second husband, Buel G. Wheeler.[66]

Markham and Cowles were members of a local circle of spiritualists hailing mainly from Austinburg, Canton, and Massillon. Some of the other members were Cornelia, Martha, and Rachel Cowles, Lorenzo Whiting, Dr. Isaac Steece from Massillon, and Louisa Austin. This circle relied on the spirit of their old friend Dr. Harry Wadsworth, who died in 1843, to send messages from the spirit world through Markham. Sometimes Wadsworth communicated with raps but more often he guided Markham's hand in writing messages from the spirit world. In this manner, Cowles received several communications from her father and from other spirits among which were Dr. Franklin Markham and Margaret Fuller.[67]

The circle's attempts to communicate with spirits were conducted in secret and all letters regarding the subject were kept confidential. "You know the ridicule wh[ich] would be heaped upon it," Cowles wrote Louisa Austin, "[and] the excitement wh[ich] would be produced; [and] it might operate against securing the communications."[68] According to Cowles, few persons were ready to accept the authenticity of spiritual manifestations. She regarded the subject of spiritualism in much the same way as she regarded abolitionism or women's rights—it was new and most people did not accept or understand new ideas. "I am not frightened because it is new," Cowles commented on the subject, "—old things were once new [and] were once disbelieved. I am far from thinking that the world is as wise now as it will be in the progress of time—hence *new things* are to come up."[69] Cowles was inclined to investigate the topic, believing in its authenticity until she was shown otherwise. She saw no reason to discount the testimonies of others whom she considered reliable.

By September 1851, spiritualism seemed to Cowles like an epidemic as strong as any religious revival. But also by that time many mediums had been exposed as fakes and some had even confessed to creating raps by temporarily displacing their joints. With these exposures, Cowles and Whiting became slightly skeptical about mediums but, nonetheless, did not discount the entire spiritual phenomenon. Concerning the circle's further investigations Cowles intimated to sisters Rachel and Cornelia:

My idea is to persevere until the thing entirely explodes or amounts to something. That it will yet arrive at some definite reliable point I am inclined to believe; at all events [I] would say *investigate,* [and] the fact that we become confounded by conflicting statements proves that the thing is not understood [and] to *intelligently condemn* we must investigate.[70]

Cowles still believed that some mediums were authentic but she and Whiting were determined to separate the false from the true manifestations. Cowles thought that time would determine whether the secret communications she received from her father through Markham were truly spiritual in nature. Learning of Cowles's belief that the message might be "humbug,"[71] Markham refused to transmit further spiritual communications to her. Not particularly upset by the medium's typical stubborn behavior, Cowles simply expected that any more messages from the deceased Wadsworth would have to come through another source.

During the course of Cowles's investigations she never regarded spiritualism as being at variance with Christianity. Rather, she believed that the spirits were enabled by God to send messages to the living in order to help them lead better lives. In an undated, private prose piece, entitled "The Departed," Cowles revealed her belief concerning the relationship between the Christian afterlife and the phenomenon of spiritualism:

'Are they [the departed] not all ministering spirits sent forth to minister to such as shall be heirs to salvation'? . . . . how can they minister unless near? They [are] near for in dreams they whisper to us 'we are here'. We see them not for the same reason that the Two, who walked . . . with their risen Lord saw him not. They felt his presence; their hearts warmed as they talked with him by the way; their spirits mingled as they communed together; but they knew him not until their eyes were opened—then they recognized and believed.

So with us—we close our ears to the gentle whisperings of love wh[ich] so oft comes to soothe us in sorrow; or to woo us from the paths of temptation—danger [and] error [and] believe not—because we cannot with the fingers of flesh feel the prints.[72]

Since Cowles believed so strongly in a Christian afterlife, but did not hold organized religions in high esteem, belief in spiritualism was a comforting alternative. Spiritualism never replaced her Christianity as a religion, but spiritualists probably seemed to Cowles much more worthy of her respect than did the leaders of some Christian sects.

Although Cowles did not state this idea specifically, she and Cornelia often exchanged scoffing or sarcastic remarks about clergymen of various sects because of their views on such reform issues as the peace cause and equal rights for women and blacks.[73] Cowles attended church services frequently; however, she did not place extreme importance on which sect's Sunday service she attended. During the late 1830s, she converted to Methodism during her stay in the Catskills, wavered back to Congregationalism during her Grand River Institute years, then adopted Presbyterianism and sometimes Methodism again during and after her years in Canton. Even when her father's old congregation in the Austinburg Congregational Church split over an organizational dispute in 1852, Cowles avoided siding with either faction in order to maintain social ties with both groups.[74]

With her weak institutional devotion, but with a strong Christian background, spiritualism fulfilled Cowles's basic belief in an afterlife and spiritual elevation. "As to bad influence," Cowles stated regarding spiritualism, "those who are engaged in the investigations are among the most spiritual [and] elevated; [and] certainly nothing in my experience has incited in me such desires for purity [and] spiritual elevation as the belief that I am in the spirit world, th'o invisible to me."[75]

Cowles's active participation in spiritual investigations continued into the late 1850s when the popular movement generally subsided in the United States. She read the *Spiritual Telegram,* the movement's major publication, and even consulted spiritual healers during her periodic trips to New York.[76]

At the Canton Union School, Cowles continued to build a lasting reputation in the teaching field in her position as superintendent of girl's grammar and high schools. Although her main subject to teach was arithmetic, she also passed along to pupils her personal sentiments concerning higher education.[77] Several of Cowles's more outgoing students even formed at her suggestion a young ladies society reminiscent of Austinburg's Young Ladies Society For Intellectual Improvement to which Cowles had belonged in the 1830's[78] Missed lovingly by dozens of Canton students during her absences in New York, Cowles returned from the city to a throng of waiting youngsters. In April 1854, Whiting described the household scene upon her return from New York:

> The Elderly critter [Cowles] has arrived at last. She has just come in & there has been a perfect storm, a tornado—a hurricane of 'young uns'

around our premises for the last half hour. I have heard nothing from her of any consequence yet. She looks well & I reckon feels well bannin [*sic*] the riding on a rail-road so long. There is not a chance to get a word in edge ways amongst these women.[79]

One Canton student composed a touching poem to the popular teacher and the lengthy piece was published in the *Ohio Repository,* a widely read paper in Canton. Indicative of the admiration and respect many students had for Cowles, the last stanza read:

> Teacher, beloved, when back we turn to thee
> Hope we'll exchange for solemn memory,
> We'll cherish in our bosom's care,
> Bright memories of the 'Days of Yore;'
> Glad hours by thee made far more bright
> Than any other transient light:
> Our fondest prayer—the boon most craved,
> Thine, a reward beyond the grave![80]

Although Cowles's pupils and Dr. Whiting were her greatest admirers, she was also popular with the Canton school's board of trustees. In September 1852, the board voted her a salary increase to four hundred dollars a year. Cowles attributed this good fortune to the fact that she had never "grumbled about it—or made them any trouble—or asked them to do it."[81] Three years later the trustees allowed Cowles to choose her own assistant since they were confident that in doing so she would keep the school's welfare in mind. The board, its spokesman informed Cowles, profoundly respected her judgment in the choice.[82] But Cowles may not have been fully satisfied with some of the board's actions since during her tenure at the Canton school the trustees administered two *coups de grace,* eliminating several of her dearest colleagues because of their religious affiliation. Purportedly, almost the entire school staff professed Presbyterianism and the board felt pressed to correct the monopoly.[83] Whether Cowles expected to lose her position or not, the weeding process disrupted the school's administration and this perhaps annoyed her.

In any event, the lure of other educational opportunities proved stronger in attracting Cowles's services than her position at Canton. Thus, in the summer of 1856, after five rewarding years, Cowles took leave of Canton, the doctor, his wife, and many devoted students.

" 'Words of cheer', yes we do need 'words of cheer'," one student wrote to Cowles after her departure,

> for you have left a void in our hearts with [*sic*] nothing but your pressence [*sic*] can fill. And . . . your name will stand engraven in characters never to be effaced, while a single heart lives in this town to record the memory of her who was beloved of all—and will I am sure, by all be deeply mourned. 'For who can fill your place deserted, who so kind, so true, so noble hearted, who.'[84]

By the time Cowles resigned from the Canton Union School in 1856, many of her peers in the teaching profession recognized the Austinburger as an outstanding and progressive educator. In that year the newly established McNeely Normal School in Hopedale, near Cadiz, Ohio, needed a talented pedagogue to head the experimental Model School. Its board of trustees unanimously chose Cowles for the position. In reporting her initial employment, the *Ohio Journal of Education,* organ of the Ohio Teacher's Association, termed Cowles a "well-known, experienced and *most accomplished*" teacher.[85] The Hopedale populace reportedly welcomed the Austinburger's experience and talent in the new institution. In August 1856, she began her new position as principal of the Model School and teacher in the Normal School.

Normal schools, or schools devoted to training teachers in their profession, were just beginning to gain public and professional support in the United States in the 1850s. By mid-century the proliferation of common schools and their organization into graded systems necessitated training teachers to a more specialized degree than in the past. Normal schools met the need for trained teachers, but they were slow to gain acceptance in the field of education. Before 1850, there were only a few such institutions in the eastern states struggling for survival, and by 1853, when the first western normal school commenced in Michigan (later Eastern Michigan University), there were only five such institutions in the United States. Normal schools multiplied during the third quarter of the nineteenth century and, by 1875, seventy state-supported normal schools from Maine to California were training approximately 23,000 teachers.[86] Thus, Cowles's association with the normal school trends, as with other new trends or movements, came at a time when its lasting acceptance was dubious and the institution itself was in an experimental stage.

The idea for a normal school in Hopedale originated with Cyrus

McNeely. He offered to grant the Ohio Teacher's Association property for such a school provided the association pledged $10,000 for its endowment. The association collected subscriptions for the project and in November 1856, the McNeely Normal School opened its doors with only a handful of students in its academic and normal departments.[87] In the spring of 1857, approximately one hundred pupils had been transfered into a Model School in which aspiring student-teachers practiced educational techniques. Cowles's job was to supervise the Model School and also teach in the normal department. Attendance wavered between fifty-six and ninety students per term. The McNeely Normal School though was financially unstable because the Ohio Teacher's Association was $3,000 short of its endowment commitment, and the school was unable to pay salaries in full. By the fall of 1857, the situation became critical. The school seemed doomed due to the association's inability to raise funds.[88] In addition to the uncertain financial security of the school, Cowles was not happy with the unsupportive attitude of the town's inhabitants and the unkept promise of the board of trustees to provide facilities for self-boarding. Cowles decided to resign. As late as 1859, the school still owed about $1,000 to its teachers for the 1857 term.[89]

Cowles's association with the McNeely Normal School ended unpleasantly, but the ordeal did not discourage her interest and support of the normal school idea. In late 1857, Charles Hovey, an ambitious Vermonter and principal of Illinois State Normal University at Bloomington, contacted Cowles about working in his newly-established institution. The Illinois State Normal University, which was a normal school elevated to the collegiate level, began its first term in October 1857. The new building was built to hold over five hundred students, but attendance the first term was an initial nineteen, rising to forty-three at the end of the term.[90] Optimistic about increasing enrollment for the second term, Hovey recruited more teachers, Cowles among them. Since Cowles, according to one of her students, was "quite extensively acquainted"[91] with most of the leading educators and principals in the Ohio school system, her reputation as a talented Ohio pedagogue probably spread to neighboring Illinois and ultimately to Charles Hovey.

Cowles accepted a position in Illinois in early 1858, but barely had time to settle in Bloomington before another more promising and attractive opportunity presented itself in Painesville, Ohio.[92] The position in Painesville was that of superintendent of the entire

Painesville public school system. Although a particularly rare position for a female to secure, Cowles's capabilities were well-known, especially in the region of northeastern Ohio. Painesville was situated on the shores of Lake Erie, not far from Austinburg. During the 1840s, Cornelia and Betsey sang in Painesville, had relatives there, and acquired numerous friends in the area.[93] Such favorable factors prompted Cowles to change jobs once again.

In the summer of 1858, the Painesville board of education officially offered the superintendency to Cowles for an annual salary of five hundred and fifty dollars per year. Before the beginning of the fall term, the *Painesville Telegraph* printed a laudatory announcement expressing "high gratification . . . in having secured the service of Miss Cowles." The news item stated further,

> She is a teacher of large experience,—has the confidence of all the leading teachers in Ohio, has been engaged in the Ohio Normal School at Hopedale, and came here from the Normal School at Bloomington, Illinois. The Board feel confident that her acknowledged ability as a teacher and still [more] in management, and [aided] by at least as able a corps of teachers as ever were in our employ, will render the present school year more pleasant and successful than any we have hitherto experienced.[94]

Built in 1831, the two-story brick building in which Cowles taught and carried out her administrative duties accommodated about two hundred grammar and high school students. Cowles boarded only a block away from the school and was frequently able to visit Austinburg, only about twenty miles away.[95] Commenting on the convenient situation, Whiting told Cowles, "I don't think you will be so used up at the end of your long terms as you used to be when you could not get away from the school at all; at any rate, not out of sight of the school rooms."[96] The doctor's comment about Cowles being "so used up" at the end of school terms reflected her desire to discontinue teaching in the not-so-distant future. Although she accepted the position in Painesville, probably because of its challenge, she thought of retiring as early as September 1858, when her first term in Painesville began. Most likely being financially stable, with over thirty years teaching experience, Cowles looked forward to the company of her sisters, friends, and family in Austinburg. Furthermore, one of her eyes began to weaken and proved troublesome during her tenure in Painesville. Perhaps suggesting that the teacher should take a rest, in January

1859, Whiting reminded her that it was of "some consequence" for her to be able to see.[97]

In October 1859, Cowles suggested to the board of education that she be replaced. The request, however, was either withdrawn or ignored since the board offered Cowles the position for the subsequent term and she took it. The following summer, however, Cowles officially notified the board of her resignation. Her successor, M. J. Oatman, received a salary of $1,000 per year, almost twice the amount Cowles received.[98] Significantly, Cowles was one of only two women ever to serve as the superintendent of Painesville school—a fact indicative of the uniqueness of her achievement in the field of education.[99]

For Cowles, the decade of the 1850s passed as the most fulfilling ten years of her life. Her battle against the Black Laws having ended shortly before the decade began, she added women's rights, spiritualism, and humanitarian works to her panorama of interests, and enjoyed multiple trips to the eastern states. She taught in no less than four different and progressive school systems and reached the pinnacle of her career in Painesville as a widely known and respected educator. Although active abolitionism took a back seat to career goals and other priorities during the 1850s, her personal concern for the welfare and ultimate fate of slaves remained strong. Toward the decade's end, as events led to the Civil War, Cowles's first and most lasting reform interest once again came to the fore.

5

The Last Years: A Conclusion

IN spite of Betsey Cowles's earlier thoughts of retirement, the Painesville superintendency was not the veteran teacher's last academic position. After her resignation from Painesville, Whiting urged Cowles to open a small school in Canton which would be less work and conveniently close to his abode.[1] The teacher was also tempted to leave retirement by a California job teaching female seminarians arranged by one of her nephews in San Francisco.[2] Instead of taking these options, by the fall of 1860, Cowles decided to yield to the lure of New York's Catskills and took a modest teaching position with the small Delhi Academy in Delhi, Delaware County, New York. Linking the Catskills with the Blue Ridge Mountains, Delaware County was hilly, mountainous in some parts, and generally a scenic spot in which to work or retire.[3] From September 1860 to March 1863, Cowles taught without notable professional incident in the New York community.

The Delhi years—Cowles's last in academia—were highlighted by the Civil War experience.[4] With the strengthening of the Republican Party in the late 1850s, many old Garrisonians broke ranks to support Abraham Lincoln's bid for the United States presidency. Cowles still believed in the original Garrisonian principle, "No Union With Slaveholders," and did not readily support the Republican Party or its candidate. One Cleveland Republican, attempting to convince her of Lincoln's good will told the unwavering Garrisonian, "While I do not say with you. 'No Union with Slaveholders' I do say most emphatically 'no compromise with slaveholders'. . . . I believe we shall not be disappointed in our man [Lincoln]."[5] Indeed, when William Lloyd Garrison began to lend the Republican Party his tacit endorsement, one of Cowles's Ashtabula County friends "suspiciouned" [sic] that Cowles might start a *Liberator* of her own.[6]

However, many of Cowles's friends and family members strongly endorsed Lincoln and the new party. Her nephew, Edwin Cowles, edited the Republican *Cleveland Leader;* and, more than once Whiting urged Cowles to leave Delhi because there she was surrounded by Breckinridge Democrats. "It seems very queer to me," he jested to Cowles, "that you are fairly well domesticated in a nest of Loco-focos! . . . [Y]ou ought to be hung for staying in such company."[7] Before the war though, Cowles did not seem greatly concerned about the kind of politics her neighbors professed.

After the Civil War began, Cowles soon became uncomfortable in the community and greatly saddened by the war.[8] She finished the 1862 school year in Delhi and then retired to Austinburg in the spring of 1863. For the remainder of the war, Cowles helped her sisters sew and prepare medical boxes for the Union troops. Her old friend Whiting was appointed to the Ohio Board of Examiners for recommending army surgeons.[9] As a long-time abolitionist and one who had extensively labored for the cause, learning of Lincoln's Emancipation Proclamation was perhaps Cowles's most lasting reward. From Delhi, some of Cowles's hometown friends supposedly heard a report that she uttered the following words after the historical document was issued: "The two great tasks of my life are ended together. My teaching is done and the slaves are free."[10]

Although the Civil War may have prompted Cowles's retirement, the main and most probable cause for ending her career was the eye trouble that had begun in Painesville. The problem worsened while she taught in Delhi during the war years. The varying diagnosis was cataracts or, at least, some kind of film on the eyes, which could be treated either medically or surgically. Cowles consulted numerous physicians concerning her condition and tried various homemade and prescribed remedies. She underwent several surgical operations in the 1860s and 1870s, but none permanently alleviated the problem or improved her failing sight.[11]

Cowles's diminishing vision, eventual "salt Rheum,"[12] and desire to spend time with the family kept her from being as active a figure in public affairs as she had been in the 1840s and 1850s. Nevertheless, after the Civil War, Cowles continued to travel and kept herself busy with community affairs until her death at home in 1876. She supported herself with the dividends from her fifty shares of stock in the *Cleveland Leader* Printing Company and the income generated from her farm property. She also received financial gifts from her nephew Alfred Cowles, business manager of the Chicago *Tribune*.[13] Her main concerns during her last decade of life were her family and the town of Austinburg. With a sense of history and sense of having made history

Betsey Mix Cowles, ca. 1860s. "My teaching is done and the slaves are free." Betsey Mix Cowles Papers. Courtesy of the American History Research Center, Kent State University Libraries.

as an early Ohio pioneer she expressed an appreciation of the heritage of Austinburg. She had incorporated many of these memories in the articles she wrote for the *Child's Friend* in the 1840s. With the passing of years her desire to preserve Austinburg's heritage grew.

Perhaps the most inspirational and personal message Cowles penned for historical reasons was the note dated 1856 she left attached to an old chest in the Cowles homestead. In its entirety it read:

> This chest was brought from Norfolk, Connecticut to Austinburg, Ohio by Joseph B. Cowles in the year 1800—was brought in an open row boat from Buffalo on Lake Erie & served as a family table for several months after the arrival of the family in this place.
>
> At the half centennial—held in Austinburg in 1850 this chest was exhibited as a relic of the early times & was given by its owner (Joseph B. Cowles) as a relic to be preserved until the centennial celebration of the settlement of the town and in it was placed the remnant of a pewter platter—several newspapers of the day—with the Ashtabula Sentinel wh. contained the account of the half centennial celebration—wh. was held in the church standing at the geographical center of the town & was the first built on the Western Reserve.
>
> These were taken charge of by Lysander M. Cowles—& by him was deposited in the house built & occupied—until his death—by Rev. Giles H. Cowles—first pastor of the Congregational Church of Austinburg.
>
> Preserve the old chest carefully for the sake of the Pioneers of the then west & if strangers—children of the present & the yet unborn shall celebrate the hundreth anniversary—spirits of the departed shall meet with them.[14]

The Austinburgers recognized Cowles's historical perspective. In 1875, after she had helped to organize the three-quarter centennial celebration of Austinburg, she was selected to preserve copies of the proceedings for reference at the centennial anniversary in 1900.[15]

The following year, 1876, the early Austinburger wrote a series of articles, entitled "Reminiscences of Olden Times" for the *Ashtabula Sentinel,* in which she recalled many of the early incidents of the town's history.[16] She related the history of the first meeting house, the first families, the first Sabbath, the frame church, and the school; the early social gatherings, early work days, and domestic customs. Cowles vividly conveyed her nostalgic sentiments in the following passage from one of her last articles:

> God Bless the matrons of those early days!
> They came "resolved each ill to bear."

O, they were brave and noble too,
Those hardy pioneers.
"They ever welcomed the stranger with sunny smiles . . ."
"Let their children arise and call them blessed."[17]

Equally indicative of Cowles's knowledge and appreciation of Austinburg's past was her service to the newly constructed Church in
acquiring memorial stained-glass windows. Each window was inscribed with the family name of the earliest town settlers. She attended to the business of providing the Congregational pastor with
the proper historical information for the windows, as well as to
writing the *Sentinel* articles in the last six months of her life.[18]

As busy as Cowles seemed to be in her later years, she was inwardly
saddened by the loss of many family members and friends. Deaths in
her immediate family included Lysander Cowles in 1857, followed by
his wife Rachel in 1859; then her youngest brother Lewis in 1861;
Cornelia Cowles in 1869; and the oldest Cowles sister, Sally, in 1872.
Dr. Whiting's wife, Mary, died in 1864. "Seventy one graves in our
family ground," Cowles sadly informed Whiting in 1872, "and five
generations are resting there."[19]

One death she particularly mourned, and a shock from which she
never fully recovered, was that of her favorite sister, Cornelia, on 6
June 1869. Cornelia was Cowles' most sympathetic and like-minded
sister in terms of women's rights, church affairs, and independent
living. Cornelia, like Cowles, never married, supported herself with a
musical and teaching career, loved to travel, and sing, and spread
abundant mirth even in her advanced years. Less than a year before
Cornelia's death, one of her friends told Betsey, "I am really spoiled
for want of one of those old side ache laughs which cannot be enjoyed
short of a visit with Cornelia—I really think she would cause a
stereotyped, fossilized presbyterian to burst his lungs . . ."[20]

Cowles missed deeply the cheerful companionship of Cornelia
since after her death the only remaining sister at home was Martha.
Cowles recorded her continuing grief over Cornelia's death in her
daily diary entries. A typical passage recorded on 23 June 1872, read,
"3 yrs 3 weeks gone gone never to return never never never" and on 29
June 1872, she entered, "3 yrs 4 weeks my heart knows the rest," and
the following day, "3 yrs 4 weeks since our great desolation. We soon
shall meet to part no more."[21]

Advancing sight loss, in addition to family deaths, also caused Cowles a great deal of inward sorrow during her last years of life. In an undated, fragmentary poem written or perhaps dictated during her sightless years, Cowles revealed the loneliness she felt:

> My father, dear father I loved so too great,
> And kind gentle mother whose voice was so [sweet],
> When they bore them away and whispered their [*sic*] dead
> I wept that my spirit with these had not fled.
> And while o'er these idols the warm tears did start.
> A voice whispered peace to the orphan's lone heart.
> It breathed of a home where the last . . . should bind
> And murmer no more, I'm blind, I'm blind.[22]

On 25 July 1876, at age sixty-six, Betsey Cowles died at the Austinburg homestead after an illness of one week. Her funeral service on the twenty-seventh was the first held in the new Congregational Church. Before her death Cowles requested that the parlor in the Austinburg homestead be maintained in the way she left it and the room remains thus preserved by her family's descendants to the present day.[23]

The worth and meaning of a single good educator may never be known except in the minds and hearts of individual students. Betsey Cowles was most certainly an extraordinarily excellent and popular educator, but the results of her vocational work are for the most part intangible. However, many praise-filled letters from her students testify to the fact that, for them, she was not just another voice in the classroom, forgotten after school's end. The story of one incident came to Cowles from Celia Dean, one of her former Delhi pupils. In 1864, Dean was teaching in the state of Iowa and discovered that one of her colleagues had been a student of Cowles in Canton. Amazed at the coincidence, and after exchanging memories with her colleague, Dean promptly sent the following message to her former teacher:

> Oh! Miss Cowles if I could only do as much good as you have done I should feel better satisfied, and I hope as you settle down to the end of your life you may have this for your consolation that you have formed many useful men and women to engage in the busy cares of life, and hope may reap your reward both here and hereafter.[24]

Harriet L. Keeler, a student of Cowles's in Delhi, became one of her most devoted friends in the 1860s and 1870s. Keeler memorialized her former teacher's life and career in a laudatory biographical sketch of Cowles in *A History of Ashtabula County* published in 1878. Notably, and perhaps as a result of her relationship with Cowles, Harriet Keeler became a prominent Cleveland educator and was president of the Cuyahoga County Women's Suffrage Party in the early twentieth century.[25]

Cowles's personal contribution to the education of American youth was, of course, only a small part of the vast educational efforts of nineteenth-century academicians. Generally, their individual and personal achievements have been unrecorded and hidden behind statistical reports, and this is especially true of the army of nineteenth-century female educators who had few other vocational opportunities.

In terms of Cowles's involvement with national trends or movements such as abolitionism and women's rights, at the local level Cowles can be considered a leader, a major participant, and a notable innovator. She had the opportunity and talent to be counted among the small group of well-known eastern female abolition leaders, but her decision to stay in the Ohio educational system prevented this possible fate. Locally, her involvement with the Ashtabula County Female Anti-Slavery Society, and the Western Anti-Slavery Society was indeed notable. Her role in the pre-Civil War women's rights movement could be qualified similarly in terms of national and local contributions.

Cowles was involved in so many activities and led such a diversely focused life that no one activity or achievement defines her overall contribution and importance to the nation's history and especially to Ohio's past. Taken as a whole, her varying degree of involvement with such new and often unpopular ideas as infant schools, normal schools, better female education, immediate abolition, women's rights, and spiritual investigations amounted to a singularly notable life's work. An Oberlin professor aptly foretold Cowles's legacy when he wrote to her in 1861, "I think of you often as providentially committed to the teacher's vocation & [you] are doing good to hundreds who are to fill their places in this active world when we shall have done filling ours."[26]

Notes

Chapter 1. The Ohio Country

References to the Cowles Family Papers are designated CFP. References to the Giles Hooker Cowles Papers are designated GHCP. References to the Betsey Mix Cowles Papers are designated BMCP.

1. Various early spellings of the family name were Cole, Coale, Coales, Cowls, and Cowles. Notably, Betsey Cowles's grandmother, Martha Hooker, was the daughter of Major Giles Hooker of Farmington, Connecticut, a lineal descendant of the Reverend Thomas Hooker, the first clergyman to settle in Connecticut in 1636. These and other details on Betsey Cowles' ancestry are found most readily in "Genealogy of the Cowles Family," Cowles Family Papers (CFP), American History Research Center, Kent State University, Kent, Ohio.

2. The most complete biographical sketch of Giles Hooker Cowles is in William W. Williams, *History of Ashtabula County, Ohio with Illustrations and Biographical Sketches of Its Pioneers and Most Prominent Men* (Philadelphia: Williams Brothers, 1878), 93–97. See also "Undated Genealogy of the Cowles Family," 9–10, and "Genealogy of the Cowles Family," CFP.

3. Epaphroditus Peck, "History of the First Congregational Church," An Historical Address Delivered October 12, 1897, in *Bristol, Connecticut (In the Olden Time "New Cambridge") Which Includes Forestville* (Hartford, Conn.: City Printing Co., 1907), 189–90.

4. Sally White was a descendant of Peregrine White, the first white child born in New England on the *Mayflower* in Cape Cod harbor. Sally's father, Lebbeus White, served under George Washington and reportedly drowned at the famous crossing of the Delaware. "Genealogy of the Cowles Family" and "Undated Genealogy of the Cowles Family," 10 (Sally White's father is listed as Alphens or Lebbeus White), CFP.

5. Sally White Cowles Dairy, 1800, Giles Hooker Cowles Papers (GHCP), American History Research Center, Kent State University, Kent, Ohio. Brief comments on Sally White appear in Williams, *History of Ashtabula County, Ohio,* 93–94.

6. "Undated Genealogy of the Cowles Family," 10, CFP. Betsey Mix Cowles probably received her middle name from an uncle, John Mix, who married Martha Cowles, a daughter of Ezekiel. Although Cowles sometimes spelled her name "Betsy," "Betsie," or "Elizabeth," she most often spelled it "Betsey." For consistency, the name will be spelled "Betsey" throughout this text.

7. Ecclesiastical Council, Bristol, Connecticut, n.d.; letter from the Monthly Convention (Canton, Conn.) recommending Giles Hooker Cowles to the People of New Connecticut, 23 May 1810, GHCP.

8. Williams, *History of Ashtabula County, Ohio,* 96; *Handbook of the First*

Congregational Church, Austinburg, Ohio (Austinburg: Howard E. Cowles Memorial Edition, 1956), 5.

9. Williams, *History of Ashtabula County, Ohio,* 95–96; *Handbook of the First Congregational Church,* 6.

10. Letter from the Monthly Convention (Canton, Conn.) recommending Giles Hooker Cowles to the People of New Connecticut, 23 May 1810; journal of missionary tour to New Connecticut, 1810, GHCP.

11. Williams, *History of Ashtabula County, Ohio,* 9–11; Henry Howe, *Historical Collections of Ohio,* 2 vols. (Norwalk, Ohio: Laning Printing Co., 1880), 1: 279; Moina W. Large, *History of Ashtabula County, Ohio,* 2 vols. (Topeka-Indianapolis: Historical Publishing Co., 1924; reprint, Cleveland: Bell & Howell Micro Photo Division), 232–34.

12. In 1800, a Deacon Noah Cowles, Lyman B. Cowles, and his wife Catherine Root Cowles, and Adna, Solomon, and Joseph B. Cowles settled in Austinburg. The Giles Hooker Cowles family of Bristol was probably related to these early Austinburg Cowles, but there is no evidence that they were in close contact before their migration. Howe, *Historical Collections* 1:279; Large, *History of Ashtabula County,* 1: 234; and lithograph of Cowles Family Tree, n.d., CFP.

13. Large, *History of Ashtabula County* 1:235–37.

14. *Handbook of the First Congregational Church,* 5–6; scrapbook article, "Reminiscences of Olden Times," 22 February 1876, Betsey Mix Cowles Papers (BMCP), American History Research Center, Kent State University, Kent, Ohio.

15. *Handbook of the First Congregational Church,* 5; scrapbook article, "Reminiscences of Olden Times," 22 February 1876, BMCP.

16. During his summer missionary tour, Giles Hooker Cowles recorded his daily undertakings in a journal. For further details of the trip refer to journal of missionary tour to New Connecticut, 1810, GHCP.

17. Williams, *History of Ashtabula County, Ohio,* 95; journal of missionary tour to New Connecticut, GHCP.

18. Williams, *History of Ashtabula County, Ohio,* 95; *Handbook of the First Congregational Church,* 6; and photocopy of a letter from Julia A. Johnson to Howard E. Cowles, 5 September 1930, BMCP (the original letter is in the possession of Margaret Cowles Ticknor, Austinburg, Ohio).

19. Journal of trip to Austinburg in Connecticut Western Reserve, May–June 1811, GHCP. The Reverend Cowles, not prolific in his journal entries, recorded only a few lines daily to describe the family's progression.

20. Journal of trip to Austinburg in Connecticut Western Reserve, GHCP.

21. Williams, *History of Ashtabula County, Ohio,* 95; *Handbook of the First Congregational Church,* 6; and scrapbook article, "Reminiscences of Olden Times," 22 February 1876, BMCP.

22. *Handbook of the First Congregational Church,* 6; Large, *History of Ashtabula County* 1:236; Williams, *History of Ashtabula County, Ohio,* 95–96; and scrapbook article, "Reminiscences of Olden Times," 22 February 1876, BMCP. The *Handbook* states that the frame church was modeled after the "Norfolk Meeting House in Litchfield County, Connecticut," while Williams states that the building was designed after a church in "Norwalk, Connecticut." The *Handbook* gives the height of the steeple as ninety-six feet, but Williams states that it was one hundred and twenty feet high.

23. Williams, *History of Ashtabula County, Ohio,* 96. This house, still standing and impressive, is now occupied by Margaret Cowles Ticknor, Giles Hooker Cowles's great-great-granddaughter.

24. Scrapbook article, "Reminiscences of Olden Times," 27 March 1876; and Simon Pure Linen Writing Tablet, (n.d.), BMCP.

25. Scrapbook article, "Reminiscences of Olden Times," 27 March 1876, BMCP; Williams, *History of Ashtabula County, Ohio*, 96.

26. Constructive legislation to provide a public school system in Ohio was not passed until 1825. The legislation in 1825 provided a tax base for common schools, established school districts and the means to elect school boards, and provided for state board of examiners to issue teacher's certificates. This legislation was not fully implemented for over a decade and, as late as 1837, there were no free public schools in Ohio outside of Cincinnati. See I. T. Frary, *Ohio in Homespun and Calico* (Richmond, Va.: Garrett and Massie, 1942), 96–106.

27. P. P. Cherry, *The Western Reserve and Early Ohio* (Akron, Ohio: R. L. Fouse, 1921), 98–103. Cherry states that students usually paid a tuition fee of fifty cents per month, but cites an example of a teacher receiving $1.00 per student for a three-month term.

28. Cherry, *Western Reserve and Early Ohio*, 101

29. Frary, *Ohio in Homespun and Calico*, 93

30. L. Cowles, Austinburg, 24 January 1823, to Cornelia [Cowles]; Martha H. Cowles, Eliza Root, and Rebecca Williams, Clinton, 20 October 1826, to Parents [Giles H. Cowles and Sally Cowles], BMCP.

31. Williams, *History of Ashtabula County, Ohio*, 100. There is no manuscript record of why Cowles abandoned her first teaching engagement. Williams states only that after one week, Cowles refused to return to the school and that ". . . sundry and divers adverse opinions concerning the desirability of school teaching" were found later in the teacher's desk. Most likely she was dissatisfied with her performance and, to this effect, Williams quotes Cowles telling novice teachers, "Now you can't possibly do worse than I did."

32. Williams, *History of Ashtabula County, Ohio*, 100. Williams is the only source that mentions Cowles teaching near Warren, Ohio. Since Williams does not mention the exact location or name of the school, further details about Cowles's engagement are not given.

33. Scrapbook article, obituary of Betsey Mix Cowles, [1876], BMCP.

34. Clifford S. Griffin, *Their Brother's Keepers: Moral Stewardship in the United States, 1800–1865* (New Brunswick, NJ: Rutgers University Press, 1960), 31, 83; receipts from the Am[erican] Ed[ucation] Society to Betsey Cowles, 3 May 1833, and 29 May 1834, BMCP.

35. Mary S. Benson, "Bethune, Joanna Graham," in Edward T. James, et al., eds., *Notable American Women 1607–1950: A Biographical Dictionary*, 3 vols. (Cambridge: Harvard University, Belknap Press, 1971), 1:138–39. Divie Bethune is discussed in Griffin, *Their Brother's Keepers*, 29, 33.

36. Isaac McIlvaine, Kinsman, 15 May 1832, to [Betsey]; Giles H. Cowles, Austinburg, 9 August 1833, to Betsey, BMCP.

37. Photocopy of Mrs. E. S. Bailey, "Infant School of 70 Years Ago," *Reminiscences* (n.p., n.d.), obtained from the Cincinnati Historical Society, Cincinnati, Ohio.

38. Record of the Literary Society of Austinburg, 1834–35, BMCP. The original thirteen members of the group were Martha and Matilda Howell, Clarinda and Mercy Austin, Mary A. Ingersoll, Betsey Lyman, Sylvia Ladd, Emily Snow, Caroline Henderson, Maria Beach, Cornelia, Rachel, and Betsey Cowles. After September 1834, young men were allowed to join.

39. Record of the Literary Society of Austinburg, 1834–35, BMCP.

40. Record of the Literary Society of Austinburg, 1834–35, BMCP; Ann Natalie Hansen, *Westward the Winds* (Columbus, Ohio: Sign of the Cock, 1974), 46.

41. Eugene Roseboom and Francis P. Weisenburger, *A History of Ohio*, 2d ed. (Columbus: Ohio Historical Society, 1976), 151–52. The American Colonization Society, formed on the Western Reserve in 1826, to send freed blacks back to Africa, proved to be a failure by 1834. Thereafter, various forms of abolitionism gained increasing popularity on the Western Reserve.

42. *Ashtabula Sentinel*, 28 April 1837.

43. *Ashtabula Sentinel*, 24 June 1834 and 19 July 1834. One Austinburger, A. E. Austin, served as recording secretary of the Ashtabula County Anti-Slavery Society in 1834, and as president of the local Colonization Society in 1835. Apparently, the ideological and practical differences between the two organizations were not clearly drawn. See *Ashtabula Sentinel*, 10 October 1835.

44. Record of the Literary Society of Austinburg, 1834–35, BMCP.

45. "Undated Genealogy of the Cowles Family," 10–14, CFP.

46. United States Census, Ashtabula County, Ohio, Austinburg Township, District No. 8, 1850, 46, American History Research Center, Kent State University, Kent, Ohio.

47. Bet [Betsey], Kinsman, 24 August [1832?], to Nelly [Cornelia Cowles], BMCP.

Chapter 2. From Granville to Oberlin

1. Griffin, *Their Brother's Keepers*, xi, 7. See also Nancy A. Hewitt, *Women's Activism and Social Change: Rochester, N.Y., 1822–1872* (Ithaca, N.Y. Cornell University Press, 1982).

2. George D. Clark, Hudson, 14 April 1836, to Sister Cowles [Betsey], BMCP.

3. Eugene Roseboom and Francis P. Weisenburger, *A History of Ohio*, 2d ed. (Columbus: Ohio Historical Society, 1976), 151–53.

4. Ibid., 151.

5. Robert Samuel Fletcher, *A History of Oberlin College*, 2 vols. (Oberlin, Ohio: Oberlin College, 1943) 1 : 144–46.

6. Roseboom and Weisenburger, *History of Ohio*, 151.

7. Russel B. Nye, *William Lloyd Garrison and the Humanitarian Reformers* (Boston: Little, Brown, 1955), 60–62.

8. Fletcher, *History of Oberlin College* 1:172–75, 183–86.

9. Douglas Andrew Gamble, "The Western Anti-Slavery Society: Garrisonian Abolitionism in Ohio" (M.A. thesis, Ohio State University, 1970), 1.

10. Robert Price, "The Ohio Anti-Slavery Convention of 1836," *The Ohio State Archaeological and Historical Quarterly* 45 (April 1936) : 186.

11. Ibid., 173–86.

12. Quoted in Aileen S. Kraditor, *Means and Ends in American Abolitionism* (New York: Pantheon, 1969), 5.

13. Ibid.

14. Williams, *History of Ashtabula County, Ohio*, 34. The original officers of the Ashtabula County (male) Anti-Slavery Society were Amos Fisk, president; Orestes K. Hawley, vice-president; and A. E. Austin, recording secretary. At the 1836 Granville meeting this society did not report the number of its members, nor the name of its president. See Price, "Ohio Anti-Slavery Convention of 1836," *OSAHQ*, 186.

15. Minute book of the Ashtabula County Anti-Slavery Society, Ashtabula County, Ohio, 1835–1837, Western Reserve Historical Society, Cleveland, Ohio. The women identified as belonging to both groups were Martha and Matilda Howell, Sylvia

Ladd, Clarinda and Mercy Austin, Caroline Henderson, and Cornelia, Rachel, and Betsey Cowles.

16. The Granville delegates praised the influence of anti-slavery women. Price states that one female employed an agent at their own expense to help organize societies in the county. The reference may have been made to Cowles's Ashtabula County Female Society which sent a Mr. Beardsley as a lecturer to various township meetings. Cowles was also instrumental in obtaining Oberlinians as lecturers. See the following correspondence: Laura M. Wright, Morgan, 1 April 1835, to Miss Cowles [Betsey]; L. [Lewis] D. Cowles, Oberlin, 30 April 1836, to Sisters [Betsey]; Maria L. Mills, Jefferson, 19 January 1836, to Miss Cowles [Betsey], BMCP.

17. Rachel A. Babcock, Wayne, 10 February 1836, to Miss Cowles [Betsey], BMCP.

18. Sarah Coleman, Andover, 11 April 1836, to Miss Cowles [Betsey], BMCP.

19. Joanna Chester, Rome, 13 April 1836, to Miss Cowles [Betsey], BMCP.

20. S. Arnold, New Lyme, 5 April [1830s?], to Betsey, BMCP.

21. Maria L. Mills, Jefferson, 19 January 1836, to Miss Cowles [Betsey], BMCP.

22. A. A. Guthrie, Putman, 9 April 1836, to Sister Cowles [Betsey], BMCP.

23. Augustus Wattles, Putman, 9 April 1836, to Sister Cowles [Betsey], BMCP.

24. Ibid.

25. Lucy M. Wright, Talmadge, 5 March 1836, to Sister [Betsey], BMCP.

26. Price, "Ohio Anti-Slavery Convention of 1836," *OSAHQ*, 186–88.

27. Lucy M. Wright, Aurora, 20 May 1836, to Sister [Betsey], BMCP. There is no evidence indicating the fate of Cowles's petition. Price does not mention the petition as being presented at the Granville meeting.

28. Copybook, "A Good Scholar," BMCP.

29. It is difficult to trace precisely Cowles's various teaching positions during the 1830s. For the most part she taught in or near Austinburg, but the time intervals varied. After her father's death in July 1835, she was employed for three months as a private tutor for several children in Hartford, Ohio.

30. Williams, *History of Ashtabula County, Ohio*, 101–102.

31. Martha Howell, Rachel, C.E.A., and Martha [Cowles], Austinburg, 29 April 1837, to Betsey, BMCP.

32. Williams, *History of Ashtabula County, Ohio*, 102.

33. Old Harry and Cornelia Cowles, Detroit, 30 January 1836, to Cousin [Betsey], BMCP.

34. Ibid.; A., Oberlin, 20 February 1836, to Cornelia [Cowles], BMCP.

35. [Cornelia Cowles], Ohio City. 31 March 1837, to Betsey, BMCP.

36. Ibid. From roughly January to April 1837, a perfectionist controversy in Austinburg was the subject of considerable discussion in the Cowles family, and the issue may have slightly facilitated Cowles's apostasy. Perfectionists believed generally that it was unacceptable morally not to go beyond ordinary Christian living toward perfect freedom from sin on earth. Nonperfectionists believed that ordinary Christian living was acceptable since perfect freedom from sin on earth was not attainable. Cornelia's opinion of the controversy was that "the grand adversary has got into both deacons," which was similar to Martha's observation that "Satan has got hold of the deacons and church." Betsey's position on the issue is unclear but such reports may have disillusioned her. S. W. Burnett, the Congregational minister who replaced the Reverend Henry Cowles after his Oberlin appointment, had considerable trouble retaining his post, apparently because of his perfectionist views. But when Austin-burgers rallied to the perfectionist banner, Burnett was allowed to stay and did so until 1841. Martha commented that if Burnett left, it would "break our society at the center," which implies that at least Martha backed Burnett's perfectionism. See the

following correspondence: Cornelia [Cowles], Ohio City, 12 January 1837, to Betsey; Eliza H. A., Sarah B. Austin, and E. Cowles, Austinburg, 15 January 1837, to Betsey; Matilda and Martha Cowles, Austinburg, 16 February 1837, to Betsey; [Cornelia Cowles], Ohio City, 31 March 1837, to Betsey; Martha Howell, Rachel, C.E.A., and Martha [Cowles], 29 April 1837, to Betsey, BMCP.

37. Matilda and Martha Cowles, Austinburg, 16 February, 1837 to Betsey; King, New York, 6 November 1837, to [Betsey], BMCP.

38. Quoted in Bertha Stearns, "Reform Periodicals and Female Reformers: 1830–1860," *American Historical Review* 37 (July 1932):683.

39. Eliza Root and Antoinette, Catskill, N.Y., 18 June 1838, to Cousins and Sisters [Betsey], BMCP.

40. Ibid.

41. M. S. Howell, Ipswich, 21 February 1835, to Betsey, BMCP.

42. Cornelia [Cowles], Ohio City, 12 January 1837, to Betsey, BMCP.

43. Williams, *History of Ashtabula County, Ohio*, 102.

44. Matilda and [Martha Cowles], Austinburg, 16 February 1837, to Betsey, BMCP.

45. Martha Howell, Matilda, and H. B. Green, Austinburg, 30 March 1837, to Betsey, BMCP.

46. [Cornelia Cowles], Ohio City, 31 March 1837, to Betsey; Lydia, Catskill, N.Y. 5 March 1838, to Friend [Betsey]; Maria P., Irvingsville, 25 March 1838, to Friend [Betsey], BMCP.

47. Fletcher, *History of Oberlin College* 1:193–94.

48. L. [Lewis] D. Cowles, Oberlin, 21 May 1835, to Sisters, [Betsey, Cornelia, and Martha], BMCP.

49. A. K. Thompson, New York, 17 August 1837, to Dear Friend [Betsey]; S. [Sarah] A. Montross, Newburg, 21 September 1837, to Cousin [Betsey]; Amelia, Flatbush, 23 September 1837, to Betsey, BMCP.

50. Martha [Cowles] and Cornelia [Cowles], n.p., July [1837?], to Betsey, BMCP.

51. Amelia, Flatbush, 23 September 1837, to Betsey, BMCP.

52. Betsey, Oberlin, 13 October 1838, to Cornelia [Cowles], BMCP.

53. James H. Fairchild, *Oberlin: The Colony and the College:1833–1883* (Oberlin, Ohio: E. J. Goodrich, 1883), 40, 41.

54. Fletcher, *History of Oberlin College* 1:190.

55. Fairchild, *Oberlin: The Colony and the College,* 177–78.

56. Fletcher, *History of Oberlin College* 1:373.

57. Ibid., 301, 307, 291.

58. Betsey, Oberlin, 13 October 1838, to Cornelia [Cowles], BMCP.

59. Ibid. For example, in an undated letter, Lovina Bissell, Austinburg abolitionist and moral reformer, chastised Cowles because her dress did not conform to their society's moral reform constitution. Bissel implied that Cowles incorrectly influenced young ladies because of her immodest dress and insobriety, meaning her mirthful character. Lovina Bissell, n.p., n.d., to Sister in the Anti-Slavery, Moral Reform, and Christian Cause [Betsey], BMCP.

60. Betsey, Oberlin, 13 October 1838, to Cornelia [Cowles], BMCP. Cowles most probably reverted to Congregationalism at Oberlin. Her supposed Methodism was not mentioned in the correspondence pertaining to Cowles's Oberlin years.

61. Ibid.

62. Ibid.

63. Betsey, Oberlin, 11 August 1839, to Sister [Cornelia], BMCP.

64. M. W. Henderson, Hudson, 19 June 1840, to Friend [Betsey], BMCP.

65. Fletcher, *History of Oberlin College* 1:303, 419, 2:899.

66. Ibid., 1:690.
67. T. [Timothy] B. Hudson, Trumbull, 11 May 1844, to Betsey, BMCP.
68. Hudson then compared their relationship to that of Titania and her "long-eared friend," Bottom, in Shakespeare's *A Midsummer Night's Dream.* In the play, Bottom, a weaver, creates a fantasy in which he poses as an ass and entices Titania to become his lover. Hudson pointed out that the comparison was not exact but that he did sometimes think of it. T. [Timothy] B. Hudson, Trumbull, 11 May 1844, to Betsey, BMCP.
69. As early as October 1840, Hudson hinted that he disapproved of Cowles's overwhelming influence on his fiancé, suggesting that when Cowles and Branch associated, they were overtaken with a "spirit of fun." He stated frankly, "I do feel that your piety is not so elevated as if you had not been together, . . . [and] I cannot conceal from myself a certain misgiving when I think of you spending the winter in each others [sic] society." Timothy B. Hudson, T. H. Fairchild and William, Oberlin, 31 October 1840, to Miss Cowles [Betsey], BMCP.
70. Fletcher, *History of Oberlin College* 1:444–5.
71. Ibid., 1:266. Fletcher states precisely that Cowles was a Garrisonian and "one of the ablest anti-slavery leaders in northern Ohio and an outstanding woman reformer in the West." Another interpretation is that Cowles was not a true Garrisonian until after her contact with Abby Kelley Foster in 1845. See Donna Marie DeBlasio, "Her Own Society: The Life and Times of Betsey Mix Cowles, 1810–1876" (Ph.D. diss., Kent State University, 1980), 50.
72. C. Preston [Martha Cowles], Betsey, and S.A.L., 8 April 1840. Austinburg, to Cornelia [Cowles], BMCP.
73. Samuel D. Cochran, Oberlin, 12 May 1840, to Miss Cowles [Betsey]; Antoinette, Austinburg, 31 July 1840, to Betsey; Timothy B. Hudson, T. H. Fairchild, and William, Oberlin, 13 October 1840, to [Betsey]; and a note on the back of [author unknown], Austinburg, 17 October 1841, to Mr. Tucker, BMCP.
74. Lindsly's first name (also spelled Lindsley) was never mentioned in the correspondence. His origin, occupation, and destiny remain a mystery.
75. Betsey, Magnolia, 16 September 1841, to Brothers and Sisters [Martha H. Cowles]; Betsey, Magnolia, 18 September 1841, to Friends [Martha H. Cowles], BMCP.
76. Betsey, Marietta, 17 November 1841, to Sisters [Martha H. Cowles], BMCP.
77. Betsey, McConnelsville, 6 December [1841?], to Brothers and Sisters [Martha H. Cowles], BMCP.
78. Betsey, Portsmouth 12 February 1842, to Sisters [Martha H. Cowles], BMCP. See also Nelson W. Evans, *A History of Scioto County, Ohio,* 2 vols. (Portsmouth, Ohio: Nelson W. Evans, 1930), 1:487–88.
79. For a short biographical sketch of Lorenzo Whiting see John H. Lehman, ed., *A Standard History of Stark County, Ohio,* 2 vols. (Chicago and New York: Lewis Publishing, [1915]), 1:170–71.
80. L. M. Whiting, Cornelia [Cowles], and Hal, Canton, 6 July 1842, to Betsey, BMCP.
81. Betsey, Portsmouth, 21 September 1842, to Sisters and Brothers. From April 1842 to April 1843, Cowles boarded with Samuel Dole, a brother of Greenleaf Dole whose death caused his wife, Salina Titcomb, to go insane. Greenleaf Dole's daughter, Selina Dole, stayed with her uncle and consequently met Betsey Cowles. Selina Dole taught in the Portsmouth public school's female department and subsequently married Lewis Cowles. Betsey, Portsmouth, 9 April 1842, to Brothers and Sisters, BMCP.
82. Betsey, Portsmouth, 21 September 1842, to Sisters and Brothers, BMCP.
83. Betsey, Portsmouth 28 September 1842, to Martha [I. Root], BMCP.

84. Margaret Hempstead, Portsmouth, 2 December 1843, to Miss Cowles [Betsey], BMCP. Similar to Cowles's concern for a Negro's right to education, was her interest in protecting fugitive slaves. From Portsmouth she learned about a slavehunter probably operating close to Austinburg and she wrote home for more information: "What was the name of the Kentuckian who was hunting slaves? From what town & Co. was he. Let me know particularly without fail; the next time any one writes!" (Betsey, Portsmouth, 28 September 1842, to Martha [I. Root], BMCP). Her interest is not surprising in light of Ashtabula County's reputation for harboring fugitive slaves on the underground railroad. The Cowles homestead in Austinburg was supposedly a station on the railroad, but there is not a word about it in the correspondence, although Lovina Bissell mentioned that her house in Austinburg was a station. Margaret Ticknor, Giles Hooker Cowles's great-great-granddaughter, lives in the Cowles homestead and possesses a rocker which she says was carried from the South by a fugitive slave and given to the Cowles sisters in appreciation for their protection (interview with Mrs. Ticknor by the author, Austinburg, 2 November 1978). In the 1930s, one of Betsey Cowles's nieces recalled, "I don't remember of hearing much about the doings of the underground railway but know that my three aunts were profoundly interested in the wellfare [sic] of the slaves and did all they could for them. But Mr. E. C. Lampson in the Jefferson *Gazette* says after a visit to the Old Cowles House, that it was one of many of the stations and that "it gave lodging to many a colored man & woman in the old garet and after nightfall they were carried to the next station on the route on the road to the lake [Erie] and Canada. . . ."

Cowles's niece noted further that the old saying used to be " 'that it was easier to get a sinner out of hell than a . . . [Negro] out of Austinburg.' " See the copy of a typescript letter written by Julia A. Cowles Johnson, Plainville, Conn., 5 September 1930, to Howard E. Cowles, BMCP. Also see Williams, *History of Ashtabula County, Ohio,* 34.

85. G. J. Leet, Lafayette, 16 April 1843, to Betsey, BMCP. Cowles could have also taken a position in Canton due to Dr. Lorenzo M. Whiting's influence with local schools, but there was not "sufficient inducement" for Cowles to teach in Canton.

Chapter 3. The Grand River Institute and Abolitionism

1. Doctor [L. M. Whiting], Canton, 3 November 1843, to Girls [Betsey or Cornelia Cowles], BMCP.

2. William W. Sweet, *Religion in the Development of American Culture, 1765–1840* (New York: Scribners, 1952; reprint, Gloucester, Mass.: Peter Smith, 1963), 164–181.

3. Williams, *History of Ashtabula County, Ohio,* 190. The ten incorporators of the Grand River Institute listed on the charter, secured on 22 February 1831, were the Reverend Giles Hooker Cowles, Moses Wilcox, Judge Eliphalet Austin, Dr. Orestes K. Hawley, Joab Austin, Joseph M. Case, Jarius Guild, Ward Childs, Gains W. St. John, and the Reverend Eliphalet Austin.

4. William H. Price's historical address in the "Report of the Proceedings of Austinburg's 75th Anniversary," [1875], newspaper clipping in scrapbook, BMCP.

5. Williams, *History of Ashtabula County, Ohio,* 190. The school's relocation, according to the *Handbook of the First Congregational Church, Austinburg,* 7, is regarded as "one of the most interesting incidents of all Austinburg history." The structure moved was a two-story building and measured approximately thirty-six by fifty feet. According to the *Handbook,* the structure's massive size necessitated the use

of one-hundred yoke of oxen to move it a distance of three miles. See also *A Grand River Album: Institute and Academy, 1831–1981* (Austinburg: Grand River Academy Sesquicentennial Committee, 1981), 10–13. This source indicates that two hundred oxen were employed in the move.

6. "Golden Years—The Semicentennial of the Founding of G.R.I.," 8 June 1882, newspaper [*Ashtabula Sentinel?*] clipping in scrapbook, BMCP.

7. *Ashtabula Sentinel,* 13 August 1840. Given that no extensive curriculum changes took place between 1840 and 1843, the 1840 *Sentinel* description roughly approximates the situation Cowles inherited in 1843.

8. "Address to an Anti-Slavery Society," n.d., BMCP. Although the address is not dated, in the text Cowles stated, "Thirteen years ago—a voice from a B. jail proclaimed the spirit of slavery." The statement most probably refers to Garrison's imprisonment in a Baltimore jail in 1830; therefore, the date of the address is probably 1843.

9. Stephen S. Foster, *The Brotherhood of Thieves; or, A True Picture of the American Church and Clergy: A Letter to Nathaniel Barney of Nantucket* (Boston: Anti-Slavery Office, 1844).

10. "Address to an Anti-Slavery Society," BMCP.

11. Theodore Dwight Weld, *American Slavery as It is: Testimony of a Thousand Witnesses* (New York: American Anti-Slavery Society, 1839).

12. "Address to an Anti-Slavery Society," BMCP.

13. Cowles may have been a member of these societies, but there are few references to them in her correspondence between 1837 and 1845.

14. References to politics occur in the following correspondence: A. D. Hawley, Austinburg, 6 July 1840, to Madam; Betsey, Portsmouth, 9 April 1842, to Brothers and Sisters [Martha H. Cowles]; Betsey, Portsmouth, 6 January 1843, to Samuel [Cowles], BMCP.

15. Alma Lutz, "Chapman, Maria Weston," Edward T. James, et al., eds., *Notable American Women* 1:224–25.

16. "Address to an Anti-Slavery Society," BMCP.

17. All quotations in this paragraph are taken from "Mission of Thought," [1840s?], BMCP.

18. Douglas Andrew Gamble, "The Western Anti-Slavery Society: Garrisonian Abolitionism in Ohio" (Master's thesis, Ohio State University, 1970), 5–13.

19. Ibid., 13. Gamble asserts that more than one-half of those present at the third anniversary meeting were influenced by Abby Kelley. Oliver Johnson, in eulogizing Kelley, maintained that the WASS would never have been organized without her efforts. See Oliver Johnson, *W. L. Garrison and His Times* (1881; reprint, Miami, Fla.: Mnemosyne, 1969), 303.

20. The *Salem Anti-Slavery Bugle* was first published on 20 June 1845, and remained the western organ for moral abolitionism until the Civil War. Although the paper was first published in New Lisbon, Ohio, it was transferred with the WASS headquarters to Salem, Ohio, in the fall of 1845. See Gamble, "The Western Anti-Slavery Society," 13–19.

21. Douglas Andrew Gamble, "Foster, Abby Kelley," *Notable American Women* 1:647. All biographical information on Foster is taken from *Notable American Women* 1:647–50.

22. For typical reactions of the press to the Fosters see the *Anti-Slavery Bugle* 14 November 1845; 21 November 1845; and 9 January 1846.

23. Johnson, *W. L. Garrison and His Times,* 303.

24. Abby K. [Kelley] Foster, Pulaski, 28 January 1846, to Friend [Betsey], BMCP.

25. [Betsey Cowles], essay, [1844–46], BMCP.

26. Betsey and Martha [Cowles], Austinburg, 3 February 1846, to Cornelia [Cowles], BMCP.

27. Cornelia Cowles, Buffalo, 1 February 1846, to Sisters and Brothers [Betsey], BMCP.

28. B. [Betsey] B. Hudson, Oberlin, 27 February 1846, to Betsey, BMCP.

29. Betsey and Martha [Cowles], Austinburg, 3 February 1846, to Cornelia [Cowles], BMCP. Although the letter is dated before the Morgan quarterly meeting, Cowles finished the letter at a later unspecified date after the Foster's departure.

30. Betsey and Martha [Cowles], Austinburg, 3 February 1846, to Cornelia [Cowles], BMCP.

31. Ibid.

32. Fletcher, *History of Oberlin College* 1:267–8.

33. B. [Betsey] B. Hudson, Oberlin, 27 February 1846, to Betsey, BMCP.

34. Ibid.

35. T. [Timothy] B. Hudson, Oberlin, 5 March 1846, to Betsey, BMCP.

36. Ibid.

37. *Anti-Slavery Bugle,* n.d., reprinted in the *Liberator,* 24 April 1846.

38. Abby K. [Kelley] Foster, Ravenna, 15 March 1846, to Friend [Betsey], BMCP.

39. *Cleveland American,* n.d., reprinted in the *Liberator,* 17 April 1846.

40. Abby K. [Kelley] Foster, Ravenna, 15 March 1846, to Friend [Betsey]; Abby K. [Kelley] F. [Foster], Randolph, 28 July [1846?], to Betsey, BMCP.

41. Mary E. Fenney, Gilmanton, 15 June 1846, to Miss Cowles [Betsey], BMCP; *Liberator,* 22 May 1846.

42. *Liberator,* 5 June 1846.

43. *Anti-Slavery Bugle,* 4 September 1846; Abby [Kelley Foster], Ravenna, 1 August 1846, to Bessy [Betsey], BMCP.

44. Abby K. [Kelley] Foster, Jefferson, 29 June 1846, to Betsey, BMCP.

45. Abby [Kelley Foster], Ravenna, 1 August 1846, to Bessy [Betsey], BMCP.

46. Abby K. [Kelley] Foster, Jefferson, 29 June 1846, to Betsey, BMCP.

47. *Anti-Slavery Bugle,* 4 September 1846.

48. Ibid., 14 August 1846.

49. Ibid., 4 September 1846.

50. Ibid.

51. J. Elizabeth Jones, Salem, 4 January 1847, to Betsey, BMCP.

52. Excerpt from *Plea for the Oppressed,* n.d., reprinted in *Anti-Slavery Bugle,* 5 March 1847.

53. Ibid.

54. Abby K. [Kelley] F. [Foster], Erie, 8 November 1846, to Betsey, BMCP.

55. Ibid.

56. Keith Melder, "Jones, Jane Elizabeth Hitchcock," *Notable American Women* 2:285–86.

57. *Anti-Slavery Bugle,* 9 April 1847; 3 September 1847; 21 April 1848.

58. Indicative of Cowles's and Jones's personal friendship see J. [Elizabeth] Jones and B. [Ben] Jones, Salem, 27 February 1848, to Betsey; Ben and Lizzie, Salem, 8 October 1847, to Betsey, BMCP.

59. Abby K. [Kelley] F. [Foster], Canterbury, 9 February 1847, to Betsey; Abby K. [Kelley] F. [Foster], Pleasantville, 2 October 1849; Abby K. [Kelley] F. [Foster], 11 November 1849, to Betsey, BMCP.

60. T. [Timothy] B. Hudson, New York, 20 January 1848, to Betsey, BMCP.

61. Sarah L. Hallowell, Rochester, 17 January 1848, to Betsey; Frederick Douglass, Rochester, 3 December 1848, to Cornelia [Cowles], BMCP.

62. Frank, Mount Pleasant, 29 August 1849, to Miss Cowles [Betsey], BMCP.

63. Samuel Dole, Portsmouth, 26 April 1850, to Nieces [Almira Dole and Selina Cowles], BMCP.

64. Rosenboom and Weisenburger, *History of Ohio*, 159–160.

65. Untitled poem beginning "Work thou on . . .," removed from diary 1842–64, BMCP.

66. *Anti-Slavery Bugle*, 26 June 1846. Cornelia Cowles also submitted an anti-war article to the *Bugle*, published on 28 January 1848.

67. Anti-war playlet with characters Uncle Sam and Zachary, n.d, BMCP. Quotations are extracted from the play's dialogue.

68. Ibid.

69. Ibid.

70. Frank, Madison, 23 November 1847, to [Betsey]; H. [Henry] C. Wright, Geneva, 3 June 1849, to Betsey, BMCP.

71. The five articles are B.M.C., "Letter to Frank," *Child's Friend and Family Magazine* 6 (September 1846): 258–61; B.M.C., "A Letter to Frank," *Child's Friend and Family Magazine* 7 (October 1846): 24–27; B.M.C., "Sunset on Lake Erie," *Child's Friend and Family Magazine* 7 (November 1846): 54–57; B.M.C., "Letter to Frank," *Child's Friend and Family Magazine* 7 (February 1847): 210–18; B.M.C., "Letter to Frank," *Child's Friend and Family Magazine* 8 (September 1847): 259–67.

72. T. [Timothy] B. Hudson, Oberlin, 5 March 1846, to Betsey, BMCP.

73. B.M.C., "Letter to Frank," *Child's Friend* 6 (September 1846): 260.

74. Ibid., 261.

75. B.M.C., "Letter to Frank," *Child's Friend* 7 (February 1847): 211.

76. B.M.C., "A Letter to Frank," *Child's Friend* 7 (October 1846): 24–27.

77. B.M.C., "Letter to Frank," *Child's Friend* 7 (February 1847): 210–18.

78. B.M.C., "Letter to Frank," *Child's Friend* 8 (September 1847): 259–67.

79. B.M.C., "Letter to Frank," *Child's Friend* 7 (February 1847): 216.

80. Ibid., 217.

81. Ibid., 217–18.

82. Lori D. Ginzberg, "Moral Suasion is Moral Balderdash: Women, Politics, and Social Activism in the 1850s," *Journal of American History* 72 (December 1986): 601–22.

Chapter 4. Women and Spirits

1. Lorenzo M. Whiting was one of Cowles's most constant correspondents from the 1840s to the 1870s. His letters as a whole convey the impressions recorded in this chapter. Letters from Whiting used as sources for specific topics or quotations will be given individual citations and such letters may be considered representative. Concerning mesmerism, see L. M. Whiting, Canton, 30 April 1843, to Roger, BMCP.

2. Doctor [L. M. Whiting], Canton, 3 November 1843, to Girls [Betsey or Cornelia Cowles]; L. M. Whiting, Canton, 12 September 1845, to C. [Cornelia Cowles], BMCP.

3. See the following letters indicative of the early Cowles-Whiting relationship: Jul, Canton, 14 January 1842, to Sister Cowles [Betsey]; Hal and Jul, Canton, 30 January 1842, to Betsey; L. M. Whiting, Canton, 19 March 1842, to Cornelia [Cowles]; C. [Cornelia] R. Cowles; Canton, 12 July 1842, to Brothers and Sisters [L. M. Cowles], BMCP.

4. C. [Cornelia] R. Cowles, Canton, 12 July 1842, to Brothers and Sisters [L. M. Cowles], BMCP.

5. L. M. Whiting, Canton 29 June 1848, to Betsey, BMCP.

6. Ibid.

7. Edward Thornton Heald, *A History of Stark County: A Digest of Mr. Heald's Six Volume Stark County Story* (Canton, Ohio: Stark County Historical Society, 1963), 21.

8. Edward H. Reisner, *The Evolution of the Common School* (New York: Macmillan, 1930), 355–57.

9. *Historical Sketches of Public Schools in Cities, Villages and Townships of the State of Ohio* (Columbus: State Centennial Education Committee, 1876), no pagination.

10. Reisner, *The Evolution of the Common School*, 384–88. Throughout the nineteenth century women teachers were usually employed to instruct lower or primary grades at a lower salary than men.

11. The act is cited in William C. Cochran, *The Western Reserve and the Fugitive Slave Law: A Prelude to the Civil War* (Cleveland, Ohio: Western Reserve Historical Society, no. 101, 1920; reprint, New York: Da Capo Press, 1972), 63–64.

12. *Anti-Slavery Bugle*, 1 December 1848.

13. *Anti-Slavery Bugle*, 2 February 1849.

14. Ibid. The Betsey Mix Cowles Papers contain a photocopy of the petition to which Cowles referred.

15. Ibid.

16. Ibid.

17. Ibid.

18. Ibid.

19. *Anti-Slavery Bugle*, 2 February 1849; Abby K. [Kelley] F. [Foster], Williamsburg, 1 October 1849, to Betsey; Abby K. [Kelley], F. [Foster], Pleasantville, 2 October 1849, to Betsey, BMCP. These are the last dated letters from Foster in the Cowles papers.

20. Copy of a letter from Betsey, New York, 24 February 1850, to Nephews and Nieces, BMCP. This letter can also be found in the Cowles-Hutchinson Letters, vol. 2, on microfilm at the American History Research Center, Kent State University, Kent, Ohio. The original volumes of the Cowles-Hutchinson Letters are in the possession of Margaret Cowles Ticknor, Austinburg, Ohio. Cornelia Cowles probably accompanied her sister on parts of the trip. See Nelly Montross, New York, 1 October 1849, to Coz, BMCP.

21. The Betsey Mix Cowles Papers contain receipts from the *Liberator* to Cowles dated from 1847 to 1865.

22. [Canton] *Ohio Repository*, 3 January 1849; 17 January 1849.

23. Ibid., 20 March 1850.

24. Betsey, Massillon, 30 November 1848, to Cornelia [Cowles], BMCP.

25. For an elementary discussion of the relationship between mesmerism and spiritualism, see Joseph McCabe, *Spiritualism: A Popular History From 1847* (New York: Dodd, Mead, 1920), 14–15; and Frank Podmore, *Mediums of the 19th Century*, vol. 1 (New Hyde Park, N.Y.: University Books, 1963), 203–205. Consult chapter 2 in McCabe and chapter 1, book 2 in Podmore for accounts of the Hydesville raps.

26. Keith E. Melder, "Jones, Jane Elizabeth Hitchcock," *Notable American Women* 2:285–86.

27. Betsey, Canton, 6 August 1850, to Louisa, BMCP.

28. Ellen C. DuBois, *Feminism and Suffrage; The Emergence of an Independent Women's Movement in America, 1848–1869* (Ithaca, N.Y.: Cornell University Press, 1978), 21–52.

29. Betsey Mix Cowles, Oberlin, 27 August 1841, to editors of the *Leader,* Cowles-Hutchinson Letters, vol. 2, American History Research Center, Kent State University.

30. Betsey, Canton, 6 August 1850, to Louisa, BMCP.

31. Eulogy for Margaret Fuller Ossoli, [1850?], BMCP.

32. Ibid.

33. Amy Clifford, "Feminism in Ohio, 1848–1857," (Master's thesis, Kent State University, 1972), 60–73.

34. *Anti-Slavery Bugle,* 30 March, 6 April, 13 April, 1850.

35. Robert W. Audretsch, comp. and ed., *The Salem, Ohio 1850 Women's Rights Convention Proceedings* (Salem, Ohio: Salem Area Bicentennial Committee and Salem Public Library, 1976), 17–20.

36. Ibid., 66.

37. Ibid., 21, 22.

38. Clifford, "Feminism in Ohio," 77, 78.

39. The entire memorial is printed in Audretsch, *The Salem . . . Proceedings,* 24–25.

40. Ibid., 52–62.

41. Ibid., 60.

42. Ibid., 22, 26–28.

43. Ibid., 66.

44. *The Proceedings of the Woman's Rights Convention, Held at Akron, Ohio, May 28 and 29, 1851* (Cincinnati, Ohio: Ben Franklin, 1851; reprint, New York: Lenox Hill, 1973), 14–20. Referring only briefly to her sources, Cowles mentioned a British government report on working women in London, "Wrongs of Women" by Charlotte Elizabeth, statistics published in the *New York Tribune,* and reports from Ashtabula County.

45. [Akron] *Proceedings. . . ,* [3], 6–8.

46. *Cleveland Herald,* n.d., as cited in the *Ashtabula Sentinel,* 21 June 1851. Cowles's report was not given any further comment in the *Sentinel,* her home-county's paper.

47. [Akron] *Proceedings. . . ,* 15.

48. Ibid. 16.

49. Ibid.

50. Ibid., 17.

51. Ibid., 19.

52. Ibid.

53. Ibid., 20.

54. Ibid.

55. Ibid., 10. The Standing Committee members were Emily Robinson of Marlboro, Cordelia L. Smalley of Randolph, Martha Tilden of Akron, Kersey G. Thomas of Marlboro, Sarah N. M'Millan of Salem, Lydia Irish of New Lisbon, and Betsey M. Cowles of Canton.

56. The proceedings of the 1852 Massillon meeting were published in the *Anti-Slavery Bugle,* 5 June 1852. Cowles is mentioned as a member of the Executive Committee. The *Bugle* does not mention Cowles in connection with women's rights business after 5 June 1852.

57. There is no solid evidence that Betsey Cowles ever adopted the Bloomer costume. However, Cowles did write a poem beginning. "Tis pleasant to canvass . . ." which contains the following lines pertaining to the garments her grandmother wore: "No outlays[,] no whalebone, no agent of Death / Were used in those garments to shorten the breath / What hardy young yeoman would look for a wife / In the form of

a woman half pressed out of life," BMCP. Thus, Cowles may have at least omitted wearing a corset.

58. Jennie M. Beckett, Massillon, 7 February 1854, to Betsey, BMCP.

59. For letters referring to Cowles's activities during the trip, see L. M. Whiting, Canton, 1 January 1854, to Betsey; I. Steece, Massillon, 14 January 1853, to Betsey; Mollie, n.p., 18 November 1853, to Teacher [Betsey]; L. M. Whiting, 29 January 1854, to Beloved [Betsey], BMCP.

60. L. M. Whiting, Canton, 11 January 1854, to Cornelia [Cowles], BMCP.

61. Betsey, New York, 21 March 1854, to Cornelia [Cowles], BMCP.

62. A Phrenological Description of the Head of Betsey Cowles, n.d., BMCP.

63. The history and development of spiritualism in Europe and in the United States is treated in Podmore, McCabe, and J. Arthur Hill, *Spiritualism Its History, Phenomena and Doctrine* (New York: George H. Doran, 1919).

64. McCabe, *Spiritualism: A Popular History*, 57.

65. Betsey, n.p., 31 March 1851, to Louisa; L.M. Whiting, Canton 29 January 1854, to Beloved [Betsey], BMCP.

66. [Helen Cowles], Cleveland, April 1843, to Aunt [Betsey], BMCP. Biographical information on Helen Cowles is taken from "Genealogy of the Cowles Family," n.d., 12, CFP.

67. Betsey, Canton, 11 September 1851, to Rachel and Cornelia [Cowles], BMCP. The original letter is in the autograph file, American History Research Center, Kent State University, Kent, Ohio. A possible spirit communication with Margaret Fuller is recorded on a fragmented, undated note beginning, "M. Preely do you know. . . .", BMCP.

68. Betsey, n.p., 31 March 1851, to Louisa, BMCP.

69. Ibid.

70. Betsey, Canton, 11 September 1851, to Rachel and Cornelia [Cowles]. Whiting reveals his skepticism in L. M. Whiting, Canton, 16 October 1851, to Cornelia [Cowles], BMCP.

71. Betsey, Canton, 11 September 1851, to Rachel and Cornelia [Cowles], BMCP.

72. Essay entitled, "The Departed," n.d., BMCP.

73. Betsey, Massillon, 30 November 1848, to Cornelia [Cowles]; Betsey, Canton, 1 December 1850, to Cornelia [Cowles]; S. Streeter, Wilton, 27 April 1872, to Friend [Betsey]; Cornelia [Cowles], Madison, Valentine's Day 1854, to Betsey, BMCP. In the latter letter, Cornelia quoted a Presbyterian preacher who stated, "Man was Lord of the Creation and God in mercy placed women in subjection." Cornelia laughed so loud at this that her companion thought she ought to be spoken to. Cornelia also called the preacher's statements against the Ohio law abolishing capital punishment "miserable twaddle." She further stated that she was so disgusted with the orthodoxy of the West and with "what stuff is inflicted upon the people" that she had to read Theodore Parker's gospel to reconcile herself to preaching again.

74. The following letters contain brief references to Cowles's religious affiliation: L. M. Whiting, Canton, 22 February 1852, to Cornelia [Cowles]; Betsey, Canton, 28 February 1852, to Cornelia [Cowles]; L. M. Whiting, Canton, 17 March 1854, to Betsey; Perkins Wallace, Canton, 28 July 1855, to Miss Cowles [Betsey]; Hattie, Closter, 26 January 1866, to Miss Cowles [Betsey]; Mary Whiting, Canton n.d., to Betsey, BMCP.

75. Betsey, n.p., 31 March to Louisa, BMCP.

76. L. M. Whiting, 29 January 1854, to Beloved [Betsey]; Oliver Johnson, New York, 31 March 1857, to Friend [Betsey]; A. W. Whiting, Canton, 17 April 1857, to Betsey; Betsey, Canton, 20 November 1852, to Louisa, BMCP.

77. Mollie, Oberlin, 17 December 1853, to Friend [Betsey]; Lizzie Albert, Can-

ton, 1854, to Miss Cowles [Betsey]; Kittie, Oberlin, 4 January 1854, to Friend [Betsey], BMCP.

78. Ann Goodman, n.p., 3 January 1854, to Teacher [Betsey], BMCP.

79. L. M. Whiting, Canton, 4 April 1854, to C. [Cornelia], BMCP.

80. Scrapbook article, "The Teacher—Her Reward," inscribed to Miss B. M. Cowles by Sarah L. Lamphear, 7 March 1856, BMCP.

81. Betsie [Betsey], Canton 20 September 1852, to Brother [Edwin Weed Cowles], Cowles-Hutchinson Letters, Vol. 3.

82. Perkins Wallace, Canton, 10 July 1855, to Betsey, BMCP.

83. Perkins Wallace, Canton, 28 July 1855, to Miss Cowles [Betsey], BMCP.

84. Henrietta Buckius, Canton, 9 July 1856, to Friend [Betsey], BMCP.

85. "The McNeely Normal School, Ohio," *Ohio Journal of Education* 6 (April 1857): 105.

86. Charles A. Harper, *A Century of Public Teacher Education* (Washington, D.C.: National Education Association, 1939), 32–35, 72.

87. Letter regarding McNeely Normal School, Athens, Ohio, 27 August 1859, BMCP.

88. "The McNeely Normal School, Ohio," *Ohio Journal of Education* 6 (April 1857): 106; [author unknown], Mansfield, 22 July 1857, to Friend [Miss Cowles], BMCP.

89. Rough typescript of a letter of resignation by Betsey Mix Cowles, n.d., original in autograph file, American History Research Center, Kent State University. Letter regarding McNeely Normal School, Athens, Ohio, 27 August 1859, BMCP. For a detailed account of the school's history and financial disposition see R. H. Eckelbery, "The McNeely Normal School and Hopedale Normal College," *Ohio State Archaelogical and Historical Quarterly* 40 (1931): 86–119.

90 Harper, *Century of Public Teacher Education*, 80–83.

91. J. S. Hunt, Hopedale, 26 December 1857, to Betsey, BMCP.

92. Correspondence relating to the Illinois State Normal University does not reveal the nature of Cowles's brief activities at the school.

93. James Cowles, Painesville, 5 May 1846, to Betsey, BMCP.

94. *Painesville Telegraph,* 26 August 1858, typescript excerpt from the Lake County Historical Society, Painesville, Ohio.

95. Records of the Educational Board of Directors of Union Schools, Town of Painesville, Lake County, State of Ohio, "Organized August 13th A.D. 1851," vol. 1, no pagination, typescript excerpts from the Lake County Historical Society.

96. L. M. Whiting, Canton, 25 September 1858, to Beloved [Betsey], BMCP.

97. [L. M. Whitting], Canton, 30 January 1859, to Betsey, BMCP.

98. Records of the Educational Board of Directors, typescript excerpt dated 3 December 1860, from the Lake County Historical Society.

99. Allen Lee Baumgartner, "A History of Public Secondary Education in Painesville, Ohio," (Master's thesis, Ohio State University, Columbus, 1936), 159, typescript excerpts from the Lake County Historical Society. Correspondence concerning Cowles's Painesville position in the Betsey Mix Cowles Papers does not reveal the reasons for her resignation. Presumably she was physically able to continue since she subsequently taught in Delhi, New York.

Chapter 5. The Last Years

1. L. M. Whiting, Canton, n.d., to Betsey, BMCP.

2. Samuel, San Francisco, 2 December 1860, to Aunt [Betsey], BMCP.

3. James Sullivan, ed., *History of New York State 1523–1927,* 3 vols. (New York: Lewis Historical Publishing, 1927) 2: 801, 804.

4. Although the Betsey Mix Cowles Papers contain no letters from Cowles regarding the John Brown incident in 1859, the collection does contain several letters to Cowles which indicate that she sympathized with Brown and was willing to aid Brown's fugitive son. Consult the following letters: Melana, n.p., 7 January 1859, to Betsey; John Brown, Jr., Dorset, 21 January 1860, to Friend [Betsey?]; W. [Wealthy] C. Brown and C. [Cornelia] R. Cowles, Dorset, 17 Mardh 1860, to Friend [Betsey]; and Melana, Austinburg, 9 April 1860, to Betsey, BMCP.

5. W. H. Price, Cleveland, 24 January 1861, to Miss Cowles, BMCP.

6. Connie Turner, Denmark, 13 February 1859, to Friend [Betsey], BMCP.

7. [L. M. Whiting], Canton, 27 January 1861, to B. [Betsey], BMCP. Although Whiting was initially troubled by the Republicans' propensity to compromise on the slavery question, he eventually supported Lincoln. See L. M. Whiting, Canton, 24 February 1861, to B. [Betsey], BMCP.

8. There are only two Civil War letters from Cowles in the Betsey Mix Cowles Papers, thus her exact thoughts and actions during the conflict are difficult to ascertain. Letters written to Cowles during the war indicate that she took an interest in the war's progress mainly as a means to end slavery. One letter to Cowles implies that she hoped for an emancipation proclamation soon after the war began and was disappointed in what she thought was Lincoln's non-moral motive for issuing one. I. Steece, Massillon, 19 October 1862, to Betsey, BMCP. Indicative of Cowles's reputation, one correspondent wrote, "Mr. Hale guesses you are fierce for this war, I told him I thought you were rather an anti-war character. [H]e said he did not care, you would make a splendid general anyhow." Connie, Akron, 29 April 1861, to Betsey, BMCP.

9. Helen, n.p., n.d., to Betsey; L. M. Whiting, Columbus, 28 April 1861, to B. [Betsey], BMCP.

10. The quote is taken from the Betsey Cowles Souvenir (Grand River Institute, 1904).

11. B. [Betsey] B. Hudson, Schodac, 12 June 1862, to Friend [Betsey]; E. P. Howard, Delhi, 25 March 1866, to Miss Cowles [Betsey]; Nelly M., New York, 13 January 1867, to Coz; Cornelia [Cowles], Austinburg, 25 June [1865–66?], to Betsey; A. [?], Massillon, 24 January 1871, to Miss Cowles, BMCP.

12. Henrietta McClurg, Union Mills, 22 October 1870, to Cousin, BMCP.

13. Will of Betsey Mix Cowles, 25 July 1876, probated 18 July 1887; A. [Alfred] Cowles, Chicago, 3 March 1873, to Betsey, BMCP.

14. Typescript of information written by Betsey Mix Cowles on lid of old chest in the Giles Hooker Cowles House, Austinburg, Ohio, dated 16 July 1856, BMCP.

15. Scrapbook article, "The Austinburg Anniversary . . . Report of the Proceedings," [1875], BMCP.

16. Scrapbook articles from 1876 dated 26 January, 22 February, 15 March, 12 April, and 3 May BMCP.

17. Scrapbook article "Reminiscences of Olden Times," 12 April 1876, BMCP.

18. J. K. Nutting, n.p., [187?], to Betsey; R. D. Whiting, Atlantic, 16 March 1876, to Betsey, BMCP.

19. L. M. Whiting, Canton, 30 October 1872, to Betsey, BMCP. Whiting quotes Cowles in the letter.

20. C. I. Bellows, Escanaba, Mich., 30 September 1868, to Friend, BMCP.

21. Diary, 1872, BMCP. Similar passages are recorded in other diaries in the Betsey Mix Cowles Papers. There is no evidence that Cowles tried to contact her dead sister through spiritualistic means.

22. Poem beginning, "I've a sweet little brother," BMCP.

23. Will of Betsey Mix Cowles, 25 July 1876, probated 18 July 1887, BMCP. Cowles willed five shares of her stock to establish a Pioneer Cemetery Fund to maintain the Pioneer Cemetery in Austinburg. For additional details concerning Cowles's post–Civil War activities see DiBlasio, "Her Own Society," 204–28.

24. Celia S. Dean, Maquoketa, Iowa, 19 September 1864, to Friend [Betsey], BMCP.

25. Ruth Neely, *Women of Ohio,* 3 vols. (Cincinnati, Ohio: S. J. Clarke Company, 1937)1: 106–107.

26. Henry Cowles, Oberlin, 11 March 1861, to Betsey, BMCP.

Bibliography

Books

Audretsch, Robert W., ed. *The Salem, Ohio 1850 Women's Rights Convention Proceedings*. Salem, Ohio: Salem Area Bicentennial Committee and Salem Public Library, 1976.

Barnes, Gilbert Hobbs. *The Anti-Slavery Impulse: 1830–1844*. New York: Appleton-Century, 1933. Reprint. Gloucester, Mass.: Peter Smith, 1957.

Bristol, Connecticut (In the Olden Time "New Cambridge") Which Includes Forestville. Hartford, Conn.: Eddy N. Smith, George Benton Smith, and Allena J. Dates, assisted by G. W. F. Blanchfield, 1907.

Brittan, S. B. and D. W. Richmond. *A Discussion of Philosophy of Ancient and Modem Spiritualism*. New York: Partridge and Brittan, 1853.

Cherry, P. P. *The Western Reserve and Early Ohio*. Akron, Ohio: R. L. Fouse, 1921.

Cochran, William C. *The Western Reserve and the Fugitive Slave Law: A Prelude to the Civil War*. Cleveland: Western Reserve Historical Society, 1920. Reprint. New York: Da Capo Press, 1972.

Cross, Whitney. *The Burned Over District: The Social and Intellectual History of Enthusiastic Religion in Western New York: 1800–1850*. New York: Harper and Row, 1950.

DuBois, Ellen Carol. *Feminism and Suffrage: The Emergence of an Independent Women's Movement in America: 1848–1869*. Ithaca, N.Y.: Cornell University Press, 1978.

Dwight, Margaret. *A Journey to Ohio in 1810*, edited by Max Farrand. New Haven: Yale University Press, 1912.

Evans, Nelson W. *A History of Scioto County, Ohio, Together with a Pioneer Record of Southern Ohio*. Privately printed, Portsmouth, Ohio: Nelson W. Evans, 1903.

Fairchild, James H. *Oberlin: The Colony and the College, 1833–1883*. Oberlin, Ohio: E. J. Goodrich, 1883.

Filler, Louis. *The Crusade Against Slavery: 1830–1860*. New American Nation Series. New York: Harper and Row, 1960.

Fletcher, Robert Samuel. *A History of Oberlin College From its Foundation Through the Civil War*. 2 vols. Oberlin, Ohio: Oberlin College, 1943.

Foster, Stephen S. *The Brotherhood of Thieves; or, a True Picture of the American Church and Clergy: A Letter to Nathaniel Barney of Nantucket*. Boston: Anti-Slavery Office, 1844.

Frary, I. T. *Ohio in Homespun and Calico*. Richmond, Va.: Garrett and Massie, 1942.

A Grand River Album: Institute and Academy: 1831–1981. [Austinburg, Ohio: Grand River Academy Sesquicentennial Committee, 1981.]

Griffin, Clifford S. *Their Brother's Keepers: Moral Stewardship in the United States, 1800–1852.* New Brunswick, N.J.: Rutgers University Press, 1960.

Hansen, Ann Natalie. *Westward the Winds; Being Some of the Main Currents of Life in Ohio: 1788–1873.* Columbus, Ohio: Sign of the Cock, 1974.

Harper, Charles A. *A Century of Public Teacher Education.* Washington, D.C.: Hugh Birch-Horace Mann Fund for the American Association of Teachers Colleges, 1939.

Heald, Edward Thornton. *A History of Stark County: A Digest of Mr. Herald's Six Volume Stark County Story.* Canton, Ohio: Stark County Historical Society, 1963.

Hewitt, Nancy A. *Women's Activism and Social Change: Rochester, New York, 1822–1872.* Ithaca, N.Y.: Cornell University Press, 1984.

Hill, J. Arthur. *Spiritualism: Its History, Phenomena and Doctrine.* New York: George H. Doran, 1919.

Hosford, Frances Juliette. *Father Shipherd's Magna Charta: A Century of Coeducation in Oberlin College.* Boston: Marshall Jones, 1937.

Howe, Henry. *Historical Collections of Ohio.* 2 vols. Norwalk: State of Ohio, 1888.

James, Edward T., et al., eds. *Notable American Women 1607–1950: A Biographical Dictionary.* 3 vols. Cambridge: Harvard University Press, Belknap Press, 1971.

Johnson, Allen, and Malone Dumas, eds. *Dictionary of American Biography.* 21 vols. New York: Scribner's 1928–37.

Johnson, Oliver. *William Lloyd Garrison and His Times: or Sketches of the Anti-Slavery Movement in America and of the Man who was its Founder and Moral Leader.* Boston: B. B. Russell, 1879. New, revised and enlarged edition. Boston: Houghton, Mifflin, 1881.

Kraditor, Aileen S. *Means and Ends in American Abolitionism: Garrison and His Critics on Strategy and Tactics, 1834–1850.* New York: Pantheon, 1967.

Large, Moina W. *History of Ashtabula County Ohio.* 2 vols. Topeka-Indianapolis: Historical Publishing Company, 1924.

Lehman, John H., ed. *A Standard History of Stark County, Ohio.* 2 vols. Chicago and New York: Lewis Publishing [1915].

Lutz, Alma *Crusade for Freedom: Women of the Anti-Slavery Movement.* Boston: Beacon Press, 1968.

Neely, Ruth. *Women of Ohio.* 3 vols. Cincinnati, Ohio: S. J. Clarke Company, 1937.

Nye, Russel B. *William Lloyd Garrison and the Humanitarian Reformers.* Boston: Little, Brown, 1955.

Podmore, Frank. *Mediums of the 19th Century.* Vol. 1. New Hyde Park, N.Y.: University Books, 1963.

Proceedings of the Woman's Rights Convention Held in Akron, Ohio, 28 and 29 May 1851. Cincinnati: Ben Franklin, 1851. Reprint. New York: Lenox Hill, 1973.

Reisner, Edward H. *The Evolution of the Common School.* New York: Macmillan, 1930.

Roseboom, Eugene, and Francis P. Weisenburger. *A History of Ohio.* 2d ed. Columbus: Ohio Historical Society, 1976.

Ruchamas, Louis. *The Abolitionists: A Collection of Their Writings.* New York: G. P. Putnam's Sons, 1963.

Sullivan, James, ed. *History of New York State: 1523–1927.* 3 vols. New York: Lewis Historical Publishing, 1927.

Sweet, William W. *Religion in the Development of American Culture, 1765–1840.* New York: Scribner's, 1952. Reprint. Gloucester, Mass.: Peter Smith, 1963.

Taylor, James W. *A Manual of the Ohio School System.* Cincinnati, Ohio: H. W. Derby, 1857.

Tyler, Alice Felt. *Freedom's Ferment: Phases of American Social History to 1860.* Minneapolis: University of Minnesota Press, 1944.

Upton, Harriet Taylor. *History of the Western Reserve.* Vol. 1. New York: Lewis Publishing, 1910.

Williams, William W. *History of Ashtabula County, Ohio, with Illustrations and Biographical Sketches of its Pioneers and Most Prominent Men.* Philadelphia: Williams Brothers, 1878.

Journal Articles

Eckelberry, R. H. "The McNeely Normal School and Hopedale Normal College." *Ohio State Archaeological and Historical Quarterly* 40 (January 1931): 86–119.

Ginzberg, Lori D. "Moral Suasion is Moral Balderdash: Women, Politics, and Social Activism in the 1850s." *Journal of American History* 73 (December 1986): 601–22.

Price, Robert. "The Ohio Anti-Slavery Convention of 1836." *Ohio State Archaeological and Historical Quarterly* 45 (April 1936): 137–88.

———. "Further Notes on Granville's Anti-Abolition Disturbances of 1836." *Ohio State Archeaological and Historical Quarterly* 45 (October 1936): 365–68.

Rosenthal, Naomi Braun. "Nineteenth Century Women in the United States: A Review Essay." *Choice* 25 (September 1987): 67–77.

Stearns, Bertha. "Reform Periodicals and Female Reformers, 1830–1860." *American Historical Review* 37 (July 1932): 678–99.

Journals

Child's Friend and Family Magazine, 1846–50.
Ohio Journal of Education, 1848–60.

Newspapers

Anti-Slavery Bugle. Salem, Ohio. 1847–60.
Ashtabula Sentinel. Jefferson, Ohio. 1832–55.
Liberator. Boston. 1843–48.
Ohio Repository. Canton, Ohio. 1850–55.
Painesville Telegraph. 1858–60. Lake County Historical Society, Painesville, Ohio.
Summit Beacon. Akron, Ohio. 1851.

Manuscripts and Typescripts

Ashtabula County Anti-Slavery Society, Minute Book, 1835–1837. Western Reserve Historical Society, Cleveland, Ohio.

Bailey, Mrs. E. S. "Infant Schools of 70 Years Ago." Excerpt from *Reminiscences,* n.d., Cincinnati Historical Society, Cincinnati, Ohio.

Baumgartner, Allen Lee. "A History of Public Secondary Education in Painesville, Ohio." Master's thesis, Ohio State University 1936.

Betsey Mix Cowles Papers. American History Research Center, Kent State University, Kent, Ohio.

Clifford, Amy H. "Feminism in Ohio, 1848–1857." Master's thesis, Kent State University, 1972.

Cowles Family Papers. American History Research Center, Kent State University, Kent, Ohio.

Cowles-Hutchinson Letters. 4 vols. Compiled by Mrs. Phillip A. Stewart (Sarah Frances Cowles), 1943. Original volumes in the possession of Margaret Cowles Ticknor, Austinburg, Ohio. Microfilm copy at the American History Research Center, Kent State University, Kent, Ohio.

DeBlasio, Donna Marie. "Her Own Society: The Life and Times of Betsey Mix Cowles, 1810–1876." Ph.D. diss., Kent State University, 1980.

Gamble, Douglas Andrew. "The Western Anti-Slavery Society: Garrisonian Abolitionism in Ohio." Master's thesis, Ohio State University, 1970.

Giles Hooker Cowles Papers. American History Research Center, Kent State University, Kent, Ohio.

Painesville, Ohio, Educational Board of Directors of Union Schools, Records. Vol. 1. Lake County Historical Society, Painesville, Ohio.

U.S. Census, Ashtabula County, Ohio. 1850. American History Research Center, Kent State University, Kent, Ohio.

Western Anti-Slavery Society (Alliance, Ohio), Minute Book, 1857–64. Western Reserve Historical Society, Cleveland, Ohio.

Index

Abolitionism: 28–29; at Oberlin College, 41–42; and women's rights, 74
Advocate of Moral Reform, 35–36, 38
American and Foreign Anti-Slavery Society, 41, 52, 61
American Anti-Slavery Society, 29; objectives of, 31; schism of, 52
American Colonization Society, 29, 100 n.41
Anti-Slavery. *See* Abolitionism
Anti-Slavery Bugle, 52, 105 n.20
Anti-Slavery Friends of Western New York, 61
Ashtabula County Anti-Slavery Society (all male), 25; officers of, 100 n.14
Ashtabula County Female Anti-Slavery Society, 25–26, 31–33, 48, 101 n.16
Ashtabula County Institute of Science and Industry. *See* Grand River Institute
Austin, Eliphalet (judge), 15, 46
Austin, Rev. Eliphalet (son), 26
Austin, Joab (merchant), 47
Austin, Lucius M. (instructor), 47
Austin, Sibbell (Mrs. Eliphalet Austin), 14, 36
Austinburg (Ohio): and anti-slavery, 205, 104 n.84; settlement of, 15–17, 19–22, 98 n.12

Badger, Rev. Joseph, 16
Bethune, Divie, 23
Bethune, Joanna Graham: and infant schools, 23–24
Black Laws, 58–59; Betsey Cowles's articles against, 69–71
Branch, Betsey (Mrs. Timothy B. Hudson), 40, 42, 55, 103 n.69
Bristol Congregational Church (Conn.), 13
Brooke, Samuel (anti-slavery agent), 57
Burnett, S. W. (pastor), 101 n.36

Canton Union School (Ohio), 84

Chapman, Maria Weston, 50–51
Child's Friend and Family Magazine, 64
Cole, John (great-great-great-grandfather), 13
Colonization Society, 29, 100 n.41
Comeouterism, 53
Congregational Church of Austinburg. *See* First Congregational Church of Austinburg
Connecticut Missionary Society, 14
Connecticut Western Reserve. *See* Western Reserve
Cowels, Samuel (great-great-grandfather), 13
Cowles, Alice Welch (Mrs. Henry Cowles), 37–38
Cowles, Betsey Mix: ancestors, 13–14, 97 n.1; anti-slavery work of, 26, 28, 31–35, 48–52, 57, 60–62, 71–72, 104 n.84; and Black Laws, 58–59, 69–71; at Canton Union School, 84–86; childhood of, 16–19, 22–25; and Civil War, 90–91, 112 n.8; at Delhi Academy (New York), 90; on education, 34, 39–40, 73; first teaching experience of, 23, 99 n.31; and Abby Kelley Foster, 54–61; at Grand River Institute, 46–48; and Timothy B. Hudson, 40–41, 55, 61, 103 nn. 68 and 69; and infant schools, 24; inheritance of, 26, 34; and Jane Elizabeth Jones, 61, 72; and "Letters to Frank," 64–66, 107 n.71; and Liberty Party, 58; at Massillon, 68–71; and Mexican War, 58, 62–63; and normal schools, 86–87; at Oberlin College, 37–42, 103 n.71; at Painesville, 88–89; at Portsmouth, 43–45, 103 n.81; religious views of, 35, 50, 84, 101 n.36; and spiritualism, 80–84; and women's rights, 73–80
Cowles, Claramond (Mrs. Lewis Cowles), 42
Cowles, Cornelia Rachel (sister): child-